IN-A-FLASH

GRAMMAR

FOR THE

TOEFL® Test

Milada Broukal

*TOEFL is a registered trademark of the Educational Testing Service, which does not endorse this book.

THOMSON

PETERSON'S

Australia • Canada • Mexico • Singapore • Spain • United Kingdom • United States

About Thomson Peterson's

Thomson Peterson's (www.petersons.com) is a leading provider of education information and advice, with books and online resources focusing on education search, test preparation, and financial aid. Its Web site offers searchable databases and interactive tools for contacting educational institutions, online practice tests and instruction, and planning tools for securing financial aid. Thomson Peterson's serves 110 million education consumers annually.

Petersons.com/publishing

Check out our Web site at www.petersons.com/publishing to see if there is any new information regarding any revisions or corrections to the content of this book. We've made sure the information in this book is accurate and up-to-date; however, the content may have changed since the time of publication.

TOEFL® and TWE® are registered trademarks of Educational Testing Service.

In-A-Flash: Grammar for the TOEFL® was adapted from *TOEFL® Test Assistant: Grammar* by Milada Broukal and published by Heinle & Heinle/ITP.

For more information, contact Thomson Peterson's, 2000 Lenox Drive, Lawrenceville, NJ 08648; 800-338-3282; or find us on the World Wide Web at www.petersons.com/about.

ISBN 0-7689-0864-7

Printed in Canada

10 9 8 7 6   06 05 04

Fourth Edition

CONTENTS

ACKNOWLEDGMENTS

I would like to thank the following professionals for their contribution by reviewing this book and giving many helpful insights and suggestions:

Paul Abraham, Simmons College
Lida Baker, University of California, Los Angeles
Kelly Franklin, Maryville College
Tom Leverett, Southern Illinois University at Carbondale
Virginia Martin, Bowling Green State University
Nancy Pfingstag, University of North Carolina at Charlotte
Bruce Rogers, Economics Institute

TO THE TEACHER

In-A-Flash: Grammar for the TOEFL® prepares students for Section 2, Structure and Written Expression, of the TOEFL® test. The text is designed for both self-study and classroom use.

The book is divided into Parts I and II. Part I includes sixteen chapters, each focusing on a grammar area tested in the Structure and Written Expression section of the test. Part II provides five Structure and Written Expression practice tests.

In Part I, the chapters are organized in order of difficulty, not according to the frequency of errors that occur on the test. However, if time is limited, the five chapters indicated below, which treat grammatical issues that most often cause errors on the TOEFL® test, can be studied first. The remaining chapters have about the same ratio of error frequency and can be studied in any order.

Chapter 15	Word Forms
Chapter 16	Word Choice and Redundancy
Chapter 4	Verbs
Chapter 13	Parallel Structure
Chapter 2	Pronouns

In each chapter the errors made in both the Structure part and the Written Expression part of the TOEFL® test are covered together. The "On the TOEFL® Test" section of each chapter gives examples of errors tested in the Structure part or the Written Expression part as they occur on the test. Also, the grammar focus exercise that follows is based on errors made in the Structure and Written Expression section.

Each chapter in Part I opens with a reading passage of general interest. The aim of this passage is to provide a context for the grammar to be discussed in the chapter as well as introduce students to the academic content areas covered in the Structure and Written Expression section. The level of difficulty in these initial passages is lower than that of the reading passages in the Vocabulary and Reading Comprehension section of the TOEFL® test, since their aim is not to improve reading skills but to provide a context for the grammar focused on in the chapter and make the grammar section of the exam more engaging and interesting for the student.

Structure of Each Chapter

INTRODUCTION

The Reading passage focuses on the grammar area of the chapter and at the same time covers a content area of the TOEFL® test through a subject of general interest. Exercises based on the reading passage introduce and reinforce the structure or grammar area covered in the chapter.

FOCUS ON GRAMMAR AREA

This part covers one of the grammar areas tested in the Structure and Written Expression section of the TOEFL® test. The examples and exercises are related in subject matter to the content area of the chapter. Strategies are given throughout this part.

ON THE TOEFL® TEST

This part focuses on the identification of errors found on the TOEFL® test, giving specific examples.

EXERCISES ON GRAMMAR FOCUS AREA

This part provides practice with TOEFL® test-type questions on the grammar area explored in the chapter. Items are in areas of mixed content.

TO THE STUDENT

Peterson's *In-A-Flash: Grammar for the TOEFL®* will prepare you for Section 2, Structure and Written Expression, of the TOEFL® test. The book is designed for both self-study and use in a classroom with a teacher. In sixteen chapters it covers all the main areas of grammar tested in this section of the test and provides you with simple explanations, TOEFL® test-type examples, and practice. For further practice there are five Structure and Written Expression practice tests in Part II of the book. You can check your answers to the chapter exercises and the practice tests using the answer key beginning on page 185.

As well as preparing you for the types of errors that are tested in the Structure and Written Expression section of the TOEFL® test, this book introduces and familiarizes you with the major content areas that appear on the TOEFL® test. These content areas are physical sciences, social sciences, and the arts and humanities.

I hope this book will make the content areas and grammar more interesting and accessible to you.

STRUCTURE AND WRITTEN EXPRESSION

The Structure and Written Expression Section of the TOEFL® Test

Section 2 of the TOEFL® test tests your understanding of English grammar. The section is divided into two parts, with a different type of question in each part:

A: Structure (questions 1-15) tests sentence completion.
B: Written Expression (questions 16-40) tests error identification.

The number of items in the Structure and Written Expression parts are as follows:

	Short Form	Long Form
Structure	15	23
Written Expression	25	37
Total	40	60
Time	25 minutes	35 minutes

- **Language:** Section 2 tests standard written English. The language in this section is more formal than the language in the Listening Comprehension section. There will be no contractions (there's) or idiomatic expressions.

- **Topics:** The topics in Section 2 are about academic subjects: the physical sciences (astronomy, geology), social sciences (anthropology, nutrition), or the arts and humanities (music, art). But you do not have to know about these subjects to answer the questions.

There are cultural references to the United States and Canada. These references may be to people, places, or things related to the United States and Canada, but you do not have to know any of these references or facts. All you have to do is concentrate on the structure of the sentence. A knowledge of the facts referred to in this section are entirely irrelevant to your score.

- **Grammar points tested:** Although a wide range of grammar points is tested, certain grammar points occur over and over again. Each chapter of this text concentrates on a particular grammar point tested on the TOEFL® test.

TACTICS

There are two ways of answering the questions appearing on the TOEFL® test.

1. *By analyzing the grammar of a sentence:* In the Structure part you can analyze the part that is missing, and in the Written Expression part the incorrect underlined item can be worked out.

2. *By using your intuition:* Some people "feel" an answer is right or wrong, although they may not know the grammar. This way may work for a person who has learned English by listening and speaking.

STRATEGIES FOR STRUCTURE AND WRITTEN EXPRESSION

- *Familiarize yourself with the directions* for both parts so you do not waste time reading the directions and examples.
- *Answer every item.* If you do not know the answer, do not leave a blank space. Always guess, even if you do not know. Wrong answers will not count against you. You can use a "guess" letter. A guess letter is one letter, A, B, C, or D, that you can use to answer all the items you do not know. You are more likely to get some correct if you use the same letter for guesses throughout the test than if you change letters all the time.
- *Use your time carefully.* Always read the four choices, even if they seem easy. You may make a careless mistake by answering a question too quickly. Don't lose time thinking about something you do not know. Mark the item lightly on your answer sheet so you can go back to it later. Go on to the next item. You should not spend more than 30 seconds per item.

Strategies for Structure: Questions 1–15

This part of the test consists of fifteen incomplete sentences. A part of each sentence is replaced by a blank. Under each sentence four choices are listed, A, B, C, and D. One of the choices logically and grammatically completes the sentence.

- *Look at the answer choices first.*

  - If they are short, you can get an idea of what to look for when you read the sentence.

  - If they are long, read the sentence (stem) first. Analyze its structure. Work out how many clauses there are. See if the clauses have subjects and verbs. Look for connectors that join the clauses. Then look at the four choices. If you still do not know the answer, eliminate as many distractors as you can and take a guess from your remaining choices.

- *Read all the choices.* Never choose an answer before reading all four choices. Some of the choices may be very similar, and you may make a careless mistake.

- *Read the sentence completely with the answer you have chosen.* Make sure your answer fits. If the answer does not sound right, it may not be. If you do not know, guess and go on. If you have time you can come back to the difficult items later.

- *Watch for the following when you insert your answer into the sentence:*

  - Your answer may have an unnecessary word or phrase.

  - It may be incomplete.

  - It may be ungrammatical. If so, discard that answer and reconsider the remaining three.

- *Use your time carefully.* Do not spend so much time that you will not have enough time to finish the Written Expression part. Budget your time carefully. Do not spend more than 30 seconds on each item.

> **Choose the one word or phrase that best completes the sentence.**

EXAMPLE I

Reflexes _____ very valuable in protecting the body against harm.

  (A) that are
  (B) being
  (C) are
  (D) are being

The best answer is (C). The sentence should read, "Reflexes are very valuable in protecting the body against harm."

EXAMPLE II

Seismographs are used to locate oil, to determine ocean depth, and _____ and measure earthquakes.

  (A) detect
  (B) to detect
  (C) be detecting
  (D) are detecting

The best answer is (B). The sentence should read, "Seismographs are used to locate oil, to determine ocean depth, and to detect and measure earthquakes."

Strategies for Written Expression: Questions 16–30

This part of the test consists of twenty-five sentences. Each sentence has four words or phrases, A, B, C, and D that are underlined. You must identify the incorrect word or phrase.

- *Read the complete sentence quickly.* Do not read just the underlined words or phrases. The underlined words or phrases may be correct on their own but incorrect in the context of the sentence.

- *The error will always be underlined.* Do not look for errors in other parts of the sentence. The rest of the sentence will only provide you with the clues to help you find the error.

- If you cannot find the error, go through a mental checklist of the most common types of errors (see the following table for a list of common errors) and see whether or not one of the underlined parts fits into one of the categories.

- If you still cannot find the error, eliminate the parts that seem correct, and then take a guess from your remaining options.

Choose the one underlined word or phrase that must be changed for the sentence to be correct.

EXAMPLE I

Navajo Indians are far more numerous today as they were in the past.
     A   B   C   D

The best answer is (C). The sentence should read, "Navajo Indians are far more numerous today than they were in the past."

EXAMPLE II

Though it is one of the rarest metals, gold was one of the first to be
  A   B   C
discover.
  D

The best answer is (D). The sentence should read, "Though it is one of the rarest metals, gold was one of the first to be discovered."

Most Common Errors in Written Expression*

Error Category	Frequency
Word form	21%
Word choice	15
Verbs	12
Parallel structure	9
Pronouns	7
Singular/plural nouns	6
Verbals (infinitives, gerunds, participles)	6
Prepositions	6
Articles	5
Comparative and superlatives	4
Word order	4
Conjunctions	2
Redundancy	1
Other types of errors	2

* Based on Bruce Roger's analysis of twenty different exams that test takers were allowed to keep after Disclosed Test Admission.

Part 1

TYPES OF STRUCTURE AND WRITTEN EXPRESSION QUESTIONS

NOUNS

Introduction: The Brain

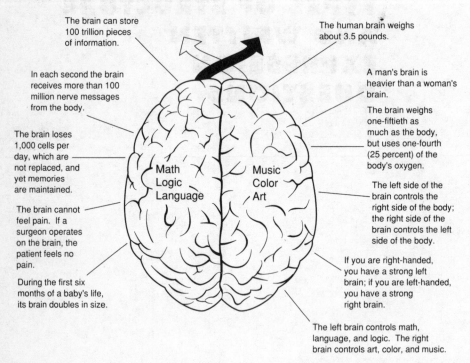

The brain can store 100 trillion pieces of information.

The human brain weighs about 3.5 pounds.

In each second the brain receives more than 100 million nerve messages from the body.

A man's brain is heavier than a woman's brain.

The brain weighs one-fiftieth as much as the body, but uses one-fourth (25 percent) of the body's oxygen.

The brain loses 1,000 cells per day, which are not replaced, and yet memories are maintained.

Math Logic Language

Music Color Art

The left side of the brain controls the right side of the body; the right side of the brain controls the left side of the body.

The brain cannot feel pain. If a surgeon operates on the brain, the patient feels no pain.

If you are right-handed, you have a strong left brain; if you are left-handed, you have a strong right brain.

During the first six months of a baby's life, its brain doubles in size.

The left brain controls math, language, and logic. The right brain controls art, color, and music.

EXERCISE 1   Answers on page 185

> ### Nouns are tested on the TOEFL® test. Complete the sentences with nouns.

1. The brain stores 100 trillion pieces of _____.

2. Men's brains are heavier than _____ brains.

3. The brain uses one quarter, or _____, of the body's oxygen.

4. The left brain controls math, _____, and _____.

5. The right brain controls color, _____, and _____.

6. The human brain weighs about 3.5 _____.

7. The brain cannot feel _____.

8. The brain receives more than 100 _____ _____ messages from the body.

EXERCISE 2   Answers on page 185

> ### From the reading, work out whether these statements are true or false. Circle T for true and F for false.

1. The weight of the brain depends on intelligence.   T F

2. A jazz musician has a dominant right brain.   T F

3. A left-handed person has a dominant left brain.   T F

4. When you play a game of chess, you use the left side of your brain.   T F

5. Your lost brain cells are always replaced.   T F

6. The brain feels pain when you have a headache.   T F

Grammar: Singular and Plural Nouns

Nouns can be classified into two groups: count nouns, which can be counted and which take an *s*, and noncount nouns, which cannot be counted and which usually do not take an *s*.

Strategy

Beware of noncount nouns that are pluralized where they generally should not be.

Look at the following table:

	Singular	**Plural**
Count noun	a cell one cell	cells two cells some cells a lot of cells many cells
Noncount noun	information some information a lot of information much information	

Count nouns
1. Take **a/an** or **one** in the singular
2. Usually take a final **s/es** in the plural

Noncount nouns
1. Do not take **a/an** in the singular
2. Do not generally have a plural form

Some count nouns are irregular and do not take an *s* in the plural. Here are some common irregular count nouns:

man—men	foot—feet
woman—women	tooth—teeth
child—children	fish—fish

Noncount nouns cannot be counted because they come in a mass or in an uncountable form. Nouns such as *blood, music,* and *excitement* cannot be counted. The following is a short list of some noncount nouns:

Food:	rice, sugar, fruit, milk, bread, butter, cheese
Fluids:	blood, water, oil, coffee, tea, gasoline
Raw materials:	wood, paper, glass, iron, silver, wool
Gases:	oxygen, nitrogen, air, pollution, steam
General:	furniture, mail, money, traffic, equipment
Groups:	jewelry, machinery, luggage, clothing, cash
Languages:	English, Chinese, Japanese, Spanish
Academic subjects:	chemistry, mathematics, psychology
Abstract things:	education, health, intelligence, beauty, knowledge, sleep, hope, music, time

QUANTIFIERS

A quantifier is a word that indicates an amount or quantity.

1. Some quantifiers are used only with plural count nouns.

   both   many   a few   several   fewer

   *They are controlled by **several** nerves.*
   *We have **fewer** cells as we get older.*

2. Some quantifiers are used only with singular count nouns.

   another   each   every

   ***Each** gland has a different purpose.*
   ***Every** muscle has its own group of nerves.*

3. Some quantifiers are used only with noncount nouns.

   a little   much   less   amount

   *The **amount** of oxygen available to the brain is important.*
   *If your brain gets **less** oxygen than it needs, you could become unconscious.*

4. Some quantifiers are used with both plural count nouns and noncount nouns.

all	plenty of	any
a lot of	enough	most
lots of	some	more

   *Brain cells use up **a lot** of energy.*
   ***Most** animals rely on instinct.*

EXERCISE 3   Answers on page 185

> ### Correct the errors in noun forms in the following sentences.

1. Intelligence is the ability to use thought and knowledges to understand things and solve problems.

2. Hormones help adjust the mixture of sugar, salt, and waters in your body.

3. Psychology, meaning the study of the mind and how it works, comes from a Greek word meaning lifes or soul.

4. Brain cells use up a lot of energy, so they need a constant supply of oxygens.

5. Each hemisphere of the brain receives informations about the opposite side of the visual field.

6. Although millions of brain neurons are active at any one time, they do not use much electric powers.

7. Lights entering the eye forms an image on 130 million tiny light cells.

8. Most animal are not able to rely on learning and memory.

COMPOUND NOUNS

> ### Strategy
>
> Beware of compound nouns in which both nouns are pluralized, instead of just the second noun.

Compound nouns are two nouns that are used together to make one word or idea. The first noun acts as an adjective to the second noun and usually does not take *s*. The second noun can be plural.

> *brain cell*
> *brain wave*
> *computer scientists*

Compound nouns may also be used with number expressions.

> **Strategy**
>
> Beware of compound nouns with numbers, where the compound noun used as an adjective may be in the plural form!

*The brain uses as much power as a **ten-watt** lightbulb.* (noun used as an adjective)

*The brain uses as much power as a lightbulb of **ten watts.*** (noun used as a noun)

*He recited a **16,000-page** book from memory.* (noun used as an adjective)

*He recited a book of **16,000 pages** from memory.* (noun used as a noun)

NUMBERS

> **Strategy**
>
> When you see nouns involving numbers, such as *hundred, thousand,* or *million,* make sure that they are not in the plural form when they follow numbers.

Numbers such as *hundred, thousand, million,* and *trillion* are plural when there are no numbers before them.

The brain receives 100 million messages a second.

The brain stores trillions of messages.

EXERCISE 4   Answers on page 185

> **Correct the errors in the following sentences.**

1. People's brains weigh more now than they did 100 year ago.
2. Nerves impulses can travel at speeds of up to 488 feet per second.
3. The brain contains between 10 trillions and 100 trillions neurons.
4. Each neuron is linked by synapses to thousand of other neurons.
5. Nerves endings below the skin's surface pick up sensations of cold, heat, and touch.
6. There are three to four millions pain receptors in the skin.
7. A three-years-old child's brain is two thirds the size it will finally be.
8. The brain uses 25 percents of the blood's oxygen.

On the TOEFL® Test

Nouns are tested in the Written Expression section of the exam. Check for the following types of errors with nouns.

1. A noncount noun may be pluralized.

   Example: In a <u>person's lifetime</u>, the brain can store <u>100 trillion</u>

   A   B
   <u>pieces</u> of <u>informations</u>.

   C   D

   The best answer is (D). *Information* is a noncount noun and cannot be plural.

2. A plural noun may be used when the verb or phrase requires a singular noun.

   Example: <u>Each part</u> of <u>the brains</u> controls <u>a separate part</u> of the

   A   B   C
   <u>body</u>.

   D

   The best answer is (B). A singular noun *brain* must be used with "part of the."

3. A singular noun may be used when the verb requires a plural noun.

   Example: Human <u>brain</u> are more powerful than those

   A
   <u>of other species</u> because of their <u>complex</u> <u>circuitry</u>.

   B   C   D

   The best answer is (A). A plural noun *brains* must be used because the verb *are* is plural.

4. In compound nouns where two nouns are used together, both nouns may be pluralized instead of just the second noun.

   Example: <u>Brains cells</u> die at the rate of <u>100,000 per day</u> by <u>age 60</u>, and

   A   B   C
   they are not replaced like <u>other body cells</u>.

   D

   The best answer is (A). The correct form is *brain cells*.

5. In compound nouns involving numbers and measurements, the compound noun used as an adjective may be in the plural form.

   Example: Man's three-pounds brain is the most complex and orderly
   <u>   A   B</u>
   <u>arrangement</u> of <u>matter</u> in the <u>universe</u>.
   <u>   C   </u>   <u>   D   </u>

   The best answer is (B). When a compound noun is used as an adjective, it is singular. Therefore the correct answer is *three-pound.*

6. When noun phrases involving a number such as *hundred, thousand,* or *million* follow another number, the plural form may be used.

   Example: The brain loses <u>fifty thousands</u> <u>neurons a day</u> and yet
   <u>   A   B   </u>
   maintains its <u>basic patterns</u> and <u>memories</u>.
   <u>   C   </u>   <u>   D   </u>

   The best answer is (A). The singular form *thousand* should be used when it follows a number.

EXERCISES ON NOUNS   Answers on page 185

> **Choose the one underlined word or phrase that must be changed for the sentence to be correct.**

1. The <u>potato</u> was the <u>staple</u> of Ireland, and when <u>the crop</u> failed in 1840,
   <u>   A   </u>   <u> B   </u>   <u>   C   </u>
   there was <u>mass starvations</u>.
   <u>   D   </u>

2. <u>Shark</u> can maneuver considerably faster than <u>other</u> <u>fish</u> because they
   <u> A </u>   <u> B </u> <u> C </u>
   <u>have no bones</u>.
   <u>   D   </u>

3. Although sugar <u>cane</u> and sugar <u>beet</u> look very different, <u>the sugars</u> that is
   <u>   A   </u>   <u> B </u>   <u>   C   </u>
   refined from them tastes almost <u>the same</u>.
   <u>   D   </u>

4. <u>Textiles industries</u> are as widespread as <u>food industries</u> because both
   <u>   A   </u>   <u>   B   </u>
   <u>supply</u> basic <u>human</u> needs.
   <u> C </u>   <u> D </u>

5. Many <u>animal species</u> are <u>totally colorsblind</u>, but <u>the condition</u> is very
   <u>   A   </u>   <u>   B   </u>   <u>   C   </u>
   rare <u>in humans</u>.
   <u>   D   </u>

6. <u>Our skulls</u> is made up of <u>eight cranial</u> and <u>fourteen</u> facial bones.
     A   B   C   D

7. <u>Diamonds</u>, which is about <u>40 times</u> as hard as <u>talc</u>, is made up of
     A   B   C
<u>pure carbon</u>.
   D

8. The oceans contain about <u>97 percent</u> of the world's <u>water supply</u>, and
     A   B   C
about another 2 percent of the world's water supply is <u>ices</u>.
                                                 D

9. <u>Brain waves patterns</u> <u>vary among</u> <u>different people</u> and in
          A   B   C
<u>different activities</u>.
   D

10. <u>The ancestor</u> of <u>today's horse</u> was a little mammal called eohippus,
      A   B
which first appeared <u>54 millions</u> <u>years ago</u>.
                      C   D

11. <u>Lasers</u> are of great value in areas such as communications, <u>industry</u>,
     A   B
<u>medicine</u>, and <u>scientifics research</u>.
   C   D

12. <u>Dinosaurs</u> are classified <u>as reptiles</u>, although <u>some appear</u> to have been
     A   B   C
<u>warms-blooded</u>.
   D

CHAPTER 2 PRONOUNS

Introduction: Penguins

There are eighteen different kinds of penguins, and they all live south of the equator. The largest are the emperor penguins, which live in Antarctica. They lay their eggs about fifty miles from the coast. There the penguins have nothing to make a nest out of, but the eggs cannot be laid directly on the ice, or they would freeze. The emperor penguins have to take care of their eggs in a special way.

The female produces one egg. As soon as she lays her egg, the male penguin rolls it on top of his feet. A special fold of skin on the bottom of his stomach comes down over the egg to protect it from the cold. For two months the male penguins stand together to protect themselves from the cold with their eggs on their feet. They cannot move or eat.

The female goes to find food as soon as she lays her egg. Finally, after two months she returns and takes the egg from the male. The male penguin, which now has had no food for two months, returns to the sea.

After the egg is hatched, the female and the male take turns carrying the baby penguin on their feet. When the weather gets cold, the baby is covered by the fold of skin, which keeps it warm.

EXERCISE 1   Answers on page 185

Pronouns are tested on the TOEFL® test. Answer the following questions in complete sentence form using a pronoun. The first one is done for you.

1. Where do the emperor penguins live?

   They live in Antarctica.

2. How many eggs does the female emperor produce at a time?

   _____

3. What does the male emperor penguin use to protect the egg from the cold?

   _____

4. Why do the male emperor penguins stand together?

   _____

5. Where do the males put their eggs when they stand together?

   _____

6. Where does the female go?

   _____

7. When does she return?

   _____

8. What does the male penguin do after she returns?

   _____

EXERCISE 2   Answers on page 185

> **From the reading, work out whether these statements are true or false. Circle T for true and F for false.**

1. There are no penguins on the North Pole.   T F

2. All penguins live south of the equator.   T F

3. All penguins are the same.   T F

4. All penguins have folds under their abdomen.   T F

5. The fold of skin is used only to keep the egg warm.   T F

6. Only the female takes care of the penguin chick.   T F

7. Emperor penguins do not make nests.   T F

8. Emperor penguins lay their eggs very near the sea.   T F

Grammar: Pronouns

There are five forms of pronouns in English: subject pronouns, object pronouns, possessive pronouns, reflexive pronouns, and relative pronouns. Possessive adjectives will also be included in this chapter, although they are not pronouns.

> **Strategy**
>
> It is important to know the five forms of pronouns and the possessive adjectives that are often confused with them. Errors may include the use of one type or form of pronoun in place of another.

SUBJECT PRONOUNS

I   we
you   you
he/she/it   they

The subject pronoun is used

- when it is the subject of a verb.
  They live south of the equator.

- when the subjects of the two clauses are compared.
  *They are more protected against the cold than **we** (are).*

- after the verb *to be*.
  *It is **he** with the egg.*

- after *as* and *than*.
  *She is not as tired as **he** (is).*

EXERCISE 3   Answers on page 185

Circle the correct pronoun.

1. It is she/her who goes to find food.
2. He/Him has the responsibility of incubating the egg.
3. She/Her lays one egg.
4. John is stronger than I/me.
5. He/Him and his father are both great explorers.
6. Are you sure that they/them are here?

OBJECT PRONOUNS

me	us
you	you
him/her/it	them

The object pronoun is used

- when it is the indirect object of a verb.

  *She gives **him** the egg.*

- after prepositions.

  *When she returns, she takes over the egg from **him.***

But when the preposition introduces a new clause, the subject pronoun must be used because the pronoun is now the subject of the new clause.

*He leaves after **she** returns.*

- when the objects of two clauses are compared.

  *It is easier for **them** than **us.***

EXERCISE 4   Answers on page 186

Correct the pronoun errors in the following sentences where necessary.

1. He helps she take care of the baby penguin.

2. She lays her egg and then leaves.

3. They feed them until they can swim.

4. It is not easy for they to survive under such conditions.

5. It is harder for him than for she.

6. He goes to the sea after she returns.

POSSESSIVE ADJECTIVES

my	our
your	your
his/her/its	their

The possessive adjective is used

- to modify a noun and show ownership.

  *They lay **their** eggs about fifty miles from the coast.*

- to refer to parts of the body.

  *The male penguin rolls the egg on top of **his** feet.*

- to modify a gerund.

  *We are surprised by **their** nesting in such harsh conditions.*

EXERCISE 5   Answers on page 186

Complete the sentences with the correct pronoun.

1. She lays _____ egg.

2. He has a special fold of skin on the bottom of _____ stomach.

3. They take care of _____ young in a special way.

4. It is protected from the cold by _____ father.

5. They keep the eggs on _____ feet.

6. The male penguin looks forward to _____ coming back with food.

POSSESSIVE PRONOUNS

mine	ours
yours	yours
his/hers/its	theirs

The possessive pronoun is used

- to replace a possessive adjective and a noun.

  *She takes her turn, and he takes **his** (his turn).*

- after the verb *to be*.

  *The egg is **hers**.*

- after the preposition *of* when it means "one of many."

  *It is a habit of **theirs**.*

- to replace the second possessive adjective and noun when they are being compared.

  *Their lives seem more difficult than **ours**.*

EXERCISE 6   Answers on page 186

Circle the correct pronoun.

1. It is an experiment of his/him.

2. The Adélie penguins live in a cold climate, but the emperor penguins live in a harsher climate than them/theirs.

3. Seven nations claim that Antarctica is their/theirs.

4. The researcher in the picture is a friend of ours/us.

5. His research was good but her/hers is better.

6. Studying penguins is a hobby of mine/my.

REFLEXIVE PRONOUNS

myself	ourselves
yourself	yourselves
himself/herself/itself	themselves

The reflexive pronoun is used

- to emphasize the subject noun or pronoun it refers to and to emphasize the fact that the subject did the action alone.

  *He takes care of the egg **himself**.*
  Or: *He **himself** takes care of the egg.*

- as the object of a verb when the subject and object are the same.

  *They stand together to protect **themselves** from the cold.*

- as the object of the preposition *by* when the subject did the action alone.

*The penguin chick is unable to get food by **itself**.*

EXERCISE 7   Answers on page 186

> **Complete the sentences with the correct reflexive pronoun.**

1. Penguins push _____ along the ice using their flippers.

2. To protect _____ from the cold, the penguin has a layer of fat under its feathers.

3. The female lays her egg and walks back to the sea by _____.

4. During the two months the male penguin cannot feed _____.

5. The male penguin _____ incubates the egg.

6. Since humans do not have the insulation that penguins do, we cannot protect _____ from such temperatures without special clothing.

RELATIVE PRONOUNS

The relative pronouns in English are *who, whom, whose, which,* and *that.*

> **Strategy**
>
> It is important to make sure that the relative pronoun agrees with the subject.

Who refers to people and household animals.

Whom refers to people and household animals. It is used in the object position in formal written English or with *who* plus a preposition in spoken English.

Whose refers to people, animals, and things. It shows possession.

Which refers to things, collective nouns, and animals.

That refers to people, animals, and things.

EXERCISE 8   Answers on page 186

Correct relative pronoun errors where necessary in the following sentences.

1. There are eighteen different kinds of penguins whom live south of the equator.

2. The biologist which went to the South Pole is studying emperor penguins.

3. Emperor penguins survive winds who blow at speeds of up to ninety-five miles an hour in winter.

4. Emperor penguins, whose nesting ground is fifty miles inland from the coast, have a special way of incubating their eggs.

5. Emperor penguins, who are the largest among penguins, do not make nests.

6. The United States has sent researchers to Antarctica which are making experiments to measure the energy expended by emperor penguins.

On the TOEFL® Test

Pronouns are tested in the Written Expression section of the exam. Check for the following types of errors with pronouns.

1. The incorrect pronoun form or type may be used. The possessive pronoun (hers) may be used instead of the possessive adjective (her).

    Example: The young emperor chick stands in <u>front of one of</u> <u>it</u> parents

                        <u>A</u>   B   C
    <u>to be protected from</u> the cold.

        D

    The best answer is (C). The possessive form *its* must be used, not the object form.

    Example: Some penguins <u>they live</u> in <u>warmer places</u> like to make

                                 A   B
    <u>their nests</u> <u>in holes in the ground.</u>

        C   D

    The best answer is (A). The relative pronoun *that* must be used instead of the subject *they*.

2. The pronoun may not agree with the noun to which it refers.

Example: Sometimes <u>penguins slide</u> on <u>their stomachs</u>, pushing <u>itself</u>

                     A   B   C

           with <u>their flippers</u>.

                  D

The best answer is (C). The noun *penguins* is plural; therefore, the reflexive pronoun referring to penguins must also be plural. The correct answer is *themselves*.

Example: Penguins <u>have special glands</u> <u>who remove</u> salt from the

                           A   B

           water <u>they drink</u> and the food <u>they eat</u>.

                 C   D

The best answer is (B). The relative pronoun *who* refers to people. In this sentence, the referent is *glands*; therefore, *that* should be used.

3. Pronouns that are not necessary may be included.

Example: <u>The male Adélie penguin</u> <u>which may not leave</u> <u>the nest</u> until

                    A   B   C

           <u>his mate</u> returns.

              D

The best answer is (B). The relative pronoun *which* is not necessary in this sentence because there is only one verb, *leave*.

Example: <u>Under the feathers</u> is a layer of fat <u>that</u> <u>it protects</u>

                    A   B   C

           <u>the penguin</u> from the cold.

              D

The best answer is (C). The pronoun *it* is not necessary.

EXERCISES ON PRONOUNS   Answers on page 186

> **Choose the one underlined word or phrase that must be changed for the sentence to be correct.**

1. The penguin <u>chicks</u> cannot go into the water to get <u>themselves</u> own
   A B
   food until <u>they have waterproof coats</u> of feathers like <u>their parents</u>.
   C D

2. <u>Balloons</u> rise into the air because <u>they contain</u> a gas <u>who is less dense</u>,
   A B C
   or <u>lighter, than air</u>.
   D

3. The narwhal is <u>the only animal</u> in the world <u>that has</u> a tusk on
   A B
   <u>only one side</u> <u>of it</u> body.
   C D

4. Silver is too soft to use <u>by itself</u>, so <u>it is mixed</u> with <u>another metal</u> to
   A B C
   make <u>themselves harder</u>.
   D

5. Most slugs and snails <u>breathe</u> using a lung <u>that opens</u> through a small
   A B
   hole <u>in the side</u> <u>of its</u> bodies.
   C D

6. Every fuel <u>has their</u> own particular temperature <u>at which</u> <u>it begins</u> to
   A B C D
   burn.

7. Harriet Tubman, <u>she an escaped slave</u>, led more than
   A
   <u>three hundred slaves</u> <u>to freedom</u> on the <u>Underground Railroad</u>.
   B C D

8. Dreaming, <u>like all</u> other mental processes, <u>it is</u> a product <u>of the brain</u>
   A B C
   and <u>its activity</u>.
   D

9. Snails produce <u>a colorless</u>, sticky discharge <u>that forms</u> a protective
   A B
   carpet <u>under them</u> as <u>their travel</u> along.
   C D

10. George Washington Carver <u>won international</u> fame for
                             ⎯⎯⎯⎯⎯⎯⎯⎯⎯⎯
                                 A
    his <u>agricultural research</u>, <u>who involved</u> <u>extensive work</u> with peanuts.
        ⎯⎯⎯⎯⎯⎯⎯⎯⎯⎯⎯⎯⎯⎯   ⎯⎯⎯⎯⎯⎯⎯⎯⎯   ⎯⎯⎯⎯⎯⎯⎯⎯⎯⎯⎯
                  B   C   D

11. Enzymes <u>enable the smallest virus</u> to enter <u>cells</u> <u>in order to</u>
            ⎯⎯⎯⎯⎯⎯⎯⎯⎯⎯⎯⎯⎯⎯⎯⎯⎯⎯⎯⎯⎯⎯⎯   ⎯⎯⎯⎯⎯   ⎯⎯⎯⎯⎯⎯⎯⎯⎯⎯
                        A   B   C
    <u>reproduce themselves</u>.
    ⎯⎯⎯⎯⎯⎯⎯⎯⎯⎯⎯⎯⎯⎯⎯⎯⎯⎯
              D

12. Jack London, <u>whom was known</u> for <u>his stories of Alaska</u>, <u>lived there</u>
                 ⎯⎯⎯⎯⎯⎯⎯⎯⎯⎯⎯⎯⎯⎯⎯   ⎯⎯⎯⎯⎯⎯⎯⎯⎯⎯⎯⎯⎯⎯⎯⎯⎯⎯⎯   ⎯⎯⎯⎯⎯⎯⎯⎯⎯⎯
                        A   B   C
    during the <u>Klondike gold rush</u>.
               ⎯⎯⎯⎯⎯⎯⎯⎯⎯⎯⎯⎯⎯⎯⎯⎯⎯
                        D

PARTS OF A SENTENCE

Introduction: Phyllis Wheatley

Phyllis Wheatley was kidnapped from Africa at the age of eight. She was brought to Boston in 1761, a sickly child only able to speak Senegalese. At the Boston slave market, Phyllis was purchased by John Wheatley, a tailor whose wife, impressed by the child's aptitude, taught her to speak, read, and write English.

In a few years Phyllis had also learned geography, history, and Latin and had developed a liking for classical poets such as Horace and Virgil. At the age of thirteen she wrote her first poem. It was a translation from the Latin of Ovid, and it so amazed the literary circles in Boston that they had it published. In 1768 she wrote "To the King's Most Excellent Health," and in 1772 she composed a poem to her mistress, who was so moved that she freed Phyllis and sent her to England to regain her health. In 1773 her first book of poems was published, the second volume of poetry published by a woman in America.

With the London publication of her book, *Poems on Various Subjects, Religious and Moral,* her fame spread on both sides of the Atlantic, and she became a celebrity.

EXERCISE 1   Answers on page 186

> **The various parts that make up a sentence are tested on the TOEFL® test. Underline the subject and circle the verb in the following sentences.**

1. At the Boston slave market, Phyllis was purchased by John Wheatley.
2. In a few years, Phyllis had learned geography, history, and Latin.
3. Her mistress, Mrs. Wheatley, was impressed by the child's aptitude.
4. At the age of thirteen, she wrote her first poem.
5. In 1773 her first book of poems was published.
6. With the London publication of her book, her fame spread on both sides of the Atlantic.

EXERCISE 2   Answers on page 186

> **In some of the sentences below, the verb agrees with the subject; in some sentences the verb does not agree with the subject. Write *C* for correct and *NC* for not correct.**

1. Phyllis Wheatley was kidnapped from Africa.

2. History, geography, and Latin was the subjects she learned.

3. Classical poets such as Horace and Virgil were Phyllis's favorites.

4. Phyllis was purchased by Mr. Wheatley, whose wife were impressed by her and taught her to speak English.

5. The literary circles in Boston were impressed by her poem.

6. On both sides of the Atlantic her poetry was famous.

Grammar: Parts of a Sentence

The clause has a subject and a verb. It can stand independently or alone.

- A **simple sentence** contains a single clause.

    She   wrote   a book.
    subject   *verb*   *object*

- A **compound sentence** contains two independent clauses joined by a conjunction (such as *and* or *but*).

    At age thirteen she wrote her first poem,
                independent clause
        and
    conjunction
    in 1773 she wrote her first book.
                independent clause

- A **complex sentence** contains an independent (main) clause and a dependent (subordinate) clause. The subordinate clause may be a noun clause, an adverb clause, or an adjective clause.

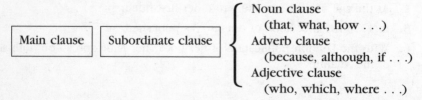

Noun clause
  (that, what, how . . .)
Adverb clause
  (because, although, if . . .)
Adjective clause
  (who, which, where . . .)

Her mistress realized <u>that Phyllis was talented.</u>
noun clause

She wrote a poem for her mistress, <u>who was very impressed</u>.
adjective clause

She went to England <u>because she had health problems</u>.
adverb clause

The three types of subordinate clauses are dealt with in Chapters 7, 8, and 9.

SUBJECT AND VERB

A clause has a subject and a verb. Some verbs (action verbs) take an object.

<u>She</u>   <u>wrote</u>   <u>a book</u>
subject   *verb*   *object*

The Verb

The verb may be a single word (*wrote* in the previous example) or a verb phrase with one or more auxiliary verbs and a main verb (*would have written*). The verb may be in active form (*wrote*) or passive form (*was written*). See Chapter 4, on verbs.

The Subject

A subject may consist of one or more nouns or a phrase:

Noun: **Phyllis** *wrote her first poem at the age of thirteen.*

Phrase: **The first black woman poet in America** *produced her first book in 1773.*

The subject may take various forms:

- A noun:

  The woman *wrote a book.*

- A pronoun:

  She *wrote a book.*

- A clause:

  What she wrote *amazed everyone.*

- A gerund:

  Writing *was her talent.*

- A gerund phrase:

  Writing poetry *was her talent.*

- An infinitive:

  To write *requires special talent.*

- An infinitive phrase:

  To write poetry *in Latin requires special talent.*

> **Strategy**
>
> There is only one subject in a clause. Be aware that on the test, the subject may be repeated. This is an error.
>
> Correct: Phyllis Wheatley wrote poetry books.
> Error: Phyllis Wheatley *she* wrote poetry books.

SUBJECT AND VERB AGREEMENT

The subject and verb must agree in person and number.

> **Strategy**
>
> Subject and verb agreement often presents difficulty to some learners of English since there are some subjects that take singular verbs and others that take plural verbs.

Subjects Taking a Singular Verb

- Subjects with the following prepositional phrases take a singular verb:

as well as	together with
along with	in addition to
accompanied by	among

  *Among her works **is** "To the King's Most Excellent Health."*

- When the words below are used as subjects, they take a singular verb:

one	each	any	some	every
		plus singular noun	*plus singular noun*	
nobody	either	anybody	somebody	everybody
no one	neither	anyone	someone	everyone
nothing		anything	something	everything

***Everyone was** amazed by her poems.*

- When *it* introduces a sentence, *it* takes a singular verb.

  ***It was** her poems that amazed everyone.*

Subjects Taking a Plural Verb

- When subjects are joined by *and* or *both . . . and,* the verb is plural.

  Both *her mother* **and** *father* **were** *proud.*

- The words *several, both, many,* and *few* always take a plural verb.

  Many *were* *amazed by her talent.*

Subjects Taking Either a Singular or a Plural Verb

- *A number of* takes a plural verb, but *the number of* takes a singular verb.

  A number of people **were** *at the reading.*
  The *number of people at the banquet* **was** *amazing.*

- The words below take a singular or plural verb depending on the noun that follows them:

none	no	all	some
most	half	any	majority

  All of her **poems were** *good.*
  All of her **work was** *good.*

- When subjects are joined by *either . . . or, neither . . . nor,* or *not only . . . but also,* the verb is singular or plural depending on the subject nearest to it.

  Not only her master but also **her mistress was** *proud of her.*
  Not only her mistress but also the literary **circles were** *amazed by her talent.*

EXERCISE 3   Answers on page 186

Choose the one word or phrase that best completes the sentence.

1. During the war _____ wrote a poem for General Washington, who complimented her on her "style and manner."
   - (A) Phyllis Wheatley was
   - (B) it was Phyllis Wheatley
   - (C) Phyllis Wheatley
   - (D) Phyllis Wheatley she

2. _____ was initially by horse or foot in the colonial period.
   - (A) It was land travel
   - (B) Land travel
   - (C) That land travel
   - (D) Because land travel

3. In 1736, the number of poor people in Boston receiving public assistance _____ about 4,000.
   - (A) was
   - (B) were
   - (C) it was
   - (D) they were

4. _____, Jupiter Hannon, was the first American black to publish his own verse.
   - (A) He was a poet and Baptist preacher of Long Island
   - (B) The poet and Baptist preacher of Long Island
   - (C) The poet and Baptist preacher of Long Island he was
   - (D) The poet and he was a Baptist preacher of Long Island

5. Outstanding for his talent as an essayist, inventor, mathematician, and astrologer in the 1770s _____, who also published a popular almanac.
   - (A) were Benjamin Banneker
   - (B) it was Benjamin Banneker
   - (C) was Benjamin Banneker
   - (D) Benjamin Banneker

6. During the eighteenth century, communication within and between cities _____ at first.
   - (A) were difficult
   - (B) they were difficult
   - (C) difficult
   - (D) was difficult

IT AND *THERE*

Strategy

Some sentences or clauses begin with *it* or *there*. Be aware of the constructions that follow these subjects. In the Structure section, parts of a sentence including *it* and *there* may be omitted.

A sentence or clause may begin with the words *it* or *there*.
It is used in three ways:

- *It* is used as subject followed by the verb *to be:*

  It was in 1761 that she came to Boston. (*It* + to be + *that*)

- *It* is used as subject when the information is related to an adjective:

  It was important to be free. (*It* + to be + adjective + infinitive)

- *It* is used as a subject when it is used with a time phrase:

  It took her a few years to learn English. (*It* + *take* + time phrase + infinitive)

There shows that something or someone exists at a special time or place. In this use, the word *there* follows this construction:

there + to be + subject

  There are many books about Phyllis Wheatley today.
  There were not many famous women poets in the 1770s.

EXERCISE 4   Answers on page 186

Circle the one word or phrase that best completes the sentence.

1. _____ not a single hard-surfaced road during the entire colonial period aside from city streets.

   (A) It was
   (B) There was
   (C) It
   (D) There were

2. _____ in 1776 that the Declaration of Independence was signed.

   (A) It was
   (B) There was
   (C) There
   (D) It

3. _____ more than 300,000 people in Philadelphia by the end of the colonial period, making it the largest city in the colonies.

(A) There was
(B) It was
(C) They were
(D) There were

4. In the eighteenth century, _____ not many women who had access to formal education in the colonies.

(A) there were
(B) it was
(C) were
(D) were there

5. After the Revolution, although some advances were made in education, _____ a slow process.

(A) they were
(B) it
(C) it was
(D) there was

On the TOEFL® Test

> Parts of a sentence are tested in the Structure section, where any part of the sentence may be missing. The subject, the verb, or both may be missing.

Example: Postal service _____ almost nonexistent in the colonies.

(A) that was
(B) was
(C) it was
(D) being

The best answer is (B). Choice (A) is incorrect because *that* is needed only to connect a relative clause to an independent clause, and in this case there is only one clause. Choice (C) is incorrect because it repeats the subject. Choice (D) is incorrect because the *-ing* form cannot be the main verb of a clause.

Example: _____ twenty-two colonial newspapers by 1775.

(A) About
(B) About were
(C) Were about
(D) There were about

The best answer is (D). Choice (A) is incorrect because it lacks a verb. Choice (B) is incorrect because there is no subject. Choice (C) is incorrect because it has the wrong word order.

EXERCISES ON PARTS OF A SENTENCE   Answers on page 187

> ## Choose the one word or phrase that best completes the sentence.

1. _____ in fluorescent lamps, television tubes, and other devices.

   (A) Phosphors are used
   (B) It is phosphors
   (C) To use phosphors
   (D) Using phosphors

2. The tips of some undersea mountains _____ islands in the middle of the ocean.

   (A) to form
   (B) they form
   (C) form
   (D) forming

3. _____ of fish: jawless fish, cartilaginous fish, and bony fish.

   (A) It is three types
   (B) There are three types
   (C) Three types
   (D) Three types are

4. _____ to stop yourself from blinking except for a short period of time.

   (A) Impossible it
   (B) Impossible
   (C) It impossible
   (D) It is impossible

5. _____ the sitka spruce a hundred years to grow eleven inches.

   (A) It takes
   (B) To take
   (C) By taking
   (D) That takes

6. _____ today was developed by the Swiss scientist Horace de Sassure around 1773.

   (A) Mountaineering it as we know
   (B) Mountaineering as we know it
   (C) We know mountaineering is
   (D) We know there is mountaineering

7. _____ of the surface of the Earth is covered by water.

   (A) Three quarters is nearly
   (B) There is nearly three quarters
   (C) It is nearly three quarters
   (D) Nearly three quarters

8. By the mid-eighteenth century _____ so many new immigrants entering North America from Europe that the original colonies in the Northeast were overcrowded.

   (A) it were
   (B) were
   (C) there
   (D) there were

9. _____ not until the end of the seventeenth century that scientists began to stress the importance of experiment as a way of gaining knowledge.

(A) There was
(B) It was
(C) There
(D) It

10. _____ are the most poisonous fish in the world.

(A) There are stonefish
(B) That the stonefish
(C) They are the stonefish
(D) Stonefish

11. Seismic prospecting _____ used to map out rock structures below the ground.

(A) widely
(B) are widely
(C) is widely
(D) it is widely

12. _____ in space, a rocket has to be powerful enough to break out of the pull of the Earth's gravity.

(A) To travel
(B) It is travel
(C) That travel
(D) Travel

CHAPTER 4 · VERBS

Introduction: The Olympics

The word "olympic" comes from the name of the town Olympia in Greece, where the ancient Olympic Games were always held. The first recorded Olympic Games were held in 776 B.C.; the Games took place every fourth year after that date until they were abolished by a Roman emperor in A.D. 394.

It was not until 1875, when archeologists discovered the ruins of the Olympic Stadium in Greece, that interest in the Games was renewed. Baron Pierre de Coubertin, a French scholar and educator, proposed that the Games should be revived as an international competition to encourage both sport and world peace.

The first modern Olympic Games were held in Athens in 1896. Like their classical predecessors, the athletes were men only; women were admitted to the Games in 1900. Since that time, the Games have been held at four-year intervals as in ancient Greece. However, since de Coubertin's dream of world peace had not been realized, the two World Wars prevented the games of 1916, 1940, and 1944 from being held.

The Olympic Games have been confined to amateur athletes despite a few recent exceptions. There are pressures on the Olympic authorities to admit other professionals to the Games. Such a step would damage the entire concept of the Olympics. The following words appear on the scoreboard at every Olympic opening: "The most important thing is not to win but to take part." In contrast, the aim of every professional is to win.

EXERCISE 1   Answers on page 187

> **Verb forms are tested on the TOEFL® test. Complete the sentences with the correct form of the verb in parentheses.**

1. The word "olympic" (come) _____ from Olympia in Greece.

2. In A.D. 394, a Roman emperor (abolish) _____ the Olympic Games.

3. In 1875 archeologists (discover) _____ the ruins of the Olympic Stadium in Greece.

4. The French educator Pierre de Coubertin (propose) _____ that the Games be revived.

5. Since 1896 the Olympic Games (be held) _____ every four years with some exceptions.

6. In the Olympic Games of 1896 the athletes (be) _____ men only.

7. Women (be admitted) _____ in 1900.

EXERCISE 2   Answers on page 187

Correct the verb tenses in the following sentences where necessary.

1. The Olympics have taken place every four years between 776 B.C. and A.D. 394.

2. Women started to participate in the Games in 1900.

3. From 1896 to the present, the Olympic Games were held every four years.

4. With a few recent exceptions, professional athletes do not take part in the Olympic Games.

5. With this international competition, Pierre de Coubertin has wanted to encourage both sport and world peace.

6. In 1916, 1940, and 1944 the Olympic Games have not taken place.

Grammar: Verbs

Verbs are tested in both the Structure and the Written Expression sections of the exam.

Strategy

It is important to:

1. Recognize the verb in a sentence (the verb is the action). Words that look like verbs, such as gerunds, infinitives, and participles, are not verbs.

2. Make sure the verb agrees with the subject (see Chapter 3).

3. Make sure the tense of the verb is correct. The time words and the context will help you do this.

TENSES

The following tables review verb tenses:

Usage	Examples
Present Continuous Tense	
1. An activity that is in progress at the moment	*Mary is watching TV right now.*
2. A general activity that takes place this week, this month, or this year	*I'm training for the Olympics.*
3. Future arrangements	*I'm going to Sweden next winter.*
Simple Present Tense	
1. A habitual action	*I run every morning.*
2. A general fact	*The sun rises in the east.*
3. Future timetables	*The ticket office opens at 9:00.*
Simple Past Tense	
1. An action that began and ended at a specific time in the past	*We won a gold medal last year.*
2. An action that occurred over a period of time and was completed in the past	*She skated for fifteen years.*
3. An activity that took place regularly in the past	*She trained every morning before work.*

Usage	Examples

Past Continuous Tense

1. An interrupted action — *I was watching the Olympics on TV when he walked in.*

2. A repeated or continuous state in the past — *I was making many new friends at the Olympic Village.*

Future Tense (going to)

1. Expressing a prior plan — *My brother is going to go with me next week.*

2. Predicting something that is likely to happen in the future — *We are going to win. I know it.*

Future Tense (will)

1. Predicting something that is likely to happen in the future — *You will win the race. I know it.*

2. Expressing willingness to do something — *I will go with you if you like.*

3. Making a decision at the time of speaking — *I will call you in a few minutes then.*

Future Continuous Tense

1. An action that will be continuing at a particular time in the future — *This time next week I will be training for the race.*

Present Perfect Tense

1. An action that happened at an unspecified time in the past — *I have seen him on television.*

2. An action that has happened recently — *She has just gone out.*

3. An action that began in the past and continues in the present (usually with "for" or "since") — *She has been training for two years.*

4. Repetition of an action before now — *He has been to the Olympics several times.*

Present Perfect Continuous Tense

1. Expressing the duration of an action that began in the past and continues in the present (with "for," "since," "all morning," "all day") — *John has been swimming for 2 hours.*

Usage	Examples
2. A general action in progress recently for which no specific time is mentioned	*I have been thinking about competing next year.*
3. An action that began in the past and has just recently ended	*Have you been crying? Your eyes are red.*

Past Perfect Tense

1. A past action that occurred before another action in the past	*She had just left when I arrived there.*
2. An action that was expected to occur in the past	*I had hoped to get their decision before today.*

Past Perfect Continuous Tense

1. Expressing the duration of an activity that occurred before another action in the past year	*She had been competing for six years before she tried out for the Olympics last year.*
2. An action occurring recently before another action in the past	*He looked tired because he had been running for 6 hours.*

Future Perfect Tense

1. An action that will be completed before a particular time in the future	*By next June I will have participated in four Olympics.*

Future Perfect Continuous Tense

1. Expressing the duration of time that has occurred before a specific time in the future	*By next May I will have been training at this gym for eleven years.*

MODALS

A modal is always followed by the base form of a verb.
The following is a list of some modals:

can	may	will	shall	must	had better
could	might	would	should	have to	ought to

A modal expresses mood or attitude:

Ability:	*She **can** run in the race.*
Possibility:	*She **could** run in the race.*
	*She **might** run in the race.*
	*She **may** run in the race.*
Advisability:	*She **had better** run in the race.*
	*She **ought to** run in the race.*
	*She **should** run in the race.*

Necessity:	*She **must** run in the race.*
	*She **has to** run in the race.*
Intention:	*She **shall** run in the race.*
	*She **will** run in the race.*
Past Habit:	*She **would** run in the race.*

Strategy

Remember the correct word order for modals.

Correct word order: *She would run in the race.*
Incorrect word order: *She run would in the race.*

EXERCISE 3   Answers on page 187

Choose the one word or phrase that best completes the sentence.

1. When archeologists discovered the ruins of the Olympic Stadium, interest in the Games _____.

   (A) was renewed
   (B) were renewed
   (C) they were renewed
   (D) renewed

2. The ancient Olympic Games _____ as amateur contests, but in time became professional.

   (A) begun
   (B) began
   (C) beginning
   (D) they began

3. The Olympic Games are held every four years in a selected country, and _____ to athletes of all nations.

   (A) they are opened
   (B) are opened
   (C) they are open
   (D) it is open

4. Winning first place in an event was the only glory in the ancient Games because second and third places _____.

   (A) did not recognize
   (B) are not recognized
   (C) was not recognized
   (D) were not recognized

5. The winners received a wreath _____ from the branches of the sacred olive tree.

   (A) made
   (B) was made
   (C) making
   (D) to make

6. After more than 1500 years, Athens _____ for the site of the first modern Olympics.

   (A) were chosen
   (B) was chosen
   (C) is chosen
   (D) chosen

7. The marathon, first staged in 1896, _____ the legendary feat of a Greek soldier who carried news of victory from the battlefield at Marathon to Athens.

   (A) was commemorated
   (B) commemorate
   (C) commemorates
   (D) commemorating

8. The Olympic torch _____ throughout the Games and is then extinguished at the closing ceremony.

   (A) burning
   (B) is burned
   (C) burned
   (D) burns

PASSIVE VOICE

Strategy

A frequent error is to use an active verb instead of a passive verb or a passive verb instead of an active verb. Remember that if the subject does the action, the verb is active; if the subject receives the action, the verb is passive.

The passive is formed by *be* + a verb ending in *ed* (past participle or an irregular past participle). In a passive sentence, the object of an active verb becomes the subject of the passive verb. The passive is used when the person or the thing done is more important, or when the agent who did the action is not known.

Active: *Archeologists **discovered** the ruins.*
Passive: *The ruins **were discovered** by archeologists.*

The following table shows how to form the passive:

Active Voice	Passive Voice
The flame *opens* the Games.	The Games *are opened* by the flame.
The flame *is opening* the Games.	The Games *are being opened* by the flame.
The flame *has opened* the Games.	The Games *have been opened* by the flame.

Active Voice	Passive Voice
The flame *opened* the Games.	The Games *were opened* by the flame.
The flame *was opening* the Games.	The Games *were being opened* by the flame.
The flame *had opened* the Games.	The Games *had been opened* by the flame.
The flame *will open* the Games.	The Games *will be opened* by the flame.
The flame *is going to open* the Games.	The Games *are going to be opened* by the flame.
The flame *will have opened* the Games.	The Games *will have been opened* by the flame.

EXERCISE 4   Answers on page 187

> **Place the verbs in parentheses in passive voice to complete the following sentences.**

1. The first modern Olympic series (hold) _____ in Athens in 1896.

2. The first Olympic Village (build) _____ for the Games in 1932.

3. The Olympic flag (fly) _____ for the first time in 1920.

4. In the 1936 Olympics, the orchestra (lead) _____ by the composer Richard Strauss.

5. The Olympic Games (cancel) _____ in 1916 because of World War I.

6. The Summer Games (show) _____ on television for the first time in 1936.

GERUNDS

Strategy

A gerund, an infinitive, or a participle is a verbal, not a verb. Gerunds or infinitives can never take the place of a main verb in a sentence. When there is a verb missing in one of the test items, make sure you choose a verb and not a verbal.

The gerund is formed by adding *-ing* to the base form of a verb. The gerund is used as a noun. It can function as a subject, object, or object of a preposition.

> ***Running*** *is my favorite sport.* (subject)
> *He tried **running** faster.* (object)
> *She was afraid of **losing.*** (object of preposition)

When the gerund is the subject of the sentence, the verb is singular.

- *Gerund after Noun + Prepositions*

    The following are some nouns + prepositions that take gerunds:

choice of	excuse for	intention of
possibility of/for	reason for	method of/for

    *He has no intention of **giving up** now.*
    *There was no reason for **canceling** the race.*

- *Gerund after Adjectives + Prepositions*

    The following are some adjectives + prepositions that take the gerund:

accustomed to	afraid of	capable of
fond of	good at	interested in
successful in	tired of	

    *She is accustomed to **training** for many hours.*
    *He is good at **running** the 200-meter race.*

- *Gerunds after Verbs*

The following are some verbs that take the gerund:

admit	deny	postpone	resume
advise	discuss	practice	risk
anticipate	enjoy	quit	suggest
appreciate	excuse	recall	tolerate
avoid	finish	recommend	try
can't help	keep	regret	understand
consider	mind	resent	imagine
delay	miss	resist	

*He kept **running** until the end.*
*She enjoys **running** for competition.*

- *Gerund after Verb + Preposition (Two-Word Verbs)*

The following are some two-word verbs that take the gerund:

approve of	give up	rely on
be better off	insist on	succeed in
call for	keep on	think about
confess to	look forward to	think of
count on	object to	worry about
depend on	put off	prevent from

*He succeeded in **winning** the race.*
*She did not give up **hoping**.*

- *Gerund or Infinitive*

Some verbs can take either a gerund or an infinitive, with no difference in meaning. The following are verbs that can take either a gerund or an infinitive:

advise	dread	mean	remember
agree	forget	neglect	start
allow	hate	permit	stop
attempt	intend	plan	study
begin	leave	prefer	try
continue	like	propose	
dislike	love	regret	

*I love **to watch** the track races.*
*I love **watching** the track races.*

INFINITIVES

The infinitive is formed by adding *to* to the base form of a verb. The infinitive can be used as a noun, an adjective, or an adverb.

> ***To train*** *is hard work.* (noun)
> *She always has energy **to spend.*** (adjective)
> *He ran **to win.*** (adverb)

- ## *Verbs That Take the Infinitive*

agree	decide	hope	prepare	threaten
appear	demand	intend	pretend	tend
arrange	deserve	learn	promise	try
ask	desire	manage	refuse	volunteer
attempt	expect	mean	regret	wait
beg	fail	need	seem	want
care	forget	offer	struggle	wish
claim	hire	order		

- ## *Verb + Noun/Pronoun + Infinitive*

The following verbs can be followed by a noun/pronoun and an infinitive:

advise	convince	force	order	teach
allow	challenge	hire	permit	tell
ask	encourage	instruct	persuade	want
cause	expect	invite	remind	warn
		need	require	

> *He reminded me **to keep** calm.*
> *I taught him **to swim.***

- ## *Adjective + Infinitive*

The following are some adjectives that are followed by the infinitive:

anxious	easy	hard	ready
boring	good	pleased	strange
dangerous		prepared	usual
difficult			

> *She was anxious **to hear** the results.*
> *It is hard **to lose.***

EXERCISE 5   Answers on page 187

Choose the one word or phrase that best completes the sentence.

1. The authorities permitted women _____ in track and field events in the 1928 Winter Games.

   (A) to take part
   (B) taking part

2. Because of a lack of snow, three thousand Austrian soldiers were hired _____ in snow for the ski trails in 1964.

   (A) bringing
   (B) to bring

3. In ancient Greece it was agreed _____ wars for the Olympic Games.

   (A) to stop
   (B) stopping

4. Women were not allowed _____ in more than three events in 1932.

   (A) participating
   (B) to participate

5. The Roman Emperor Theodosius ordered the Games _____ in A.D. 394.

   (A) stopping
   (B) to stop

6. The two World Wars prevented the Olympics from _____ place.

   (A) taking
   (B) to take

On the TOEFL® Test

In the Structure section, verb errors may involve the following.

1. *A verb may not agree with its subject.* A singular subject requires a singular verb, and a plural subject requires a plural verb.

2. *A verb may be in the wrong tense.* The time words and the context will indicate the correct tense.

3. *A verb may be in the active form instead of the passive or vice versa.* If the subject does the action, the verb must be active; if the subject receives the action, the verb is passive.

4. *A verbal is not a verb.* A gerund or participle cannot be a main verb.

   Example: Electronic timing _____ for the first time in the 1912 Olympics in Sweden.
   - (A) were used
   - (B) was used
   - (C) using
   - (D) used

   The best answer is (B). Choice (A) is incorrect because the subject is in gerund form and therefore requires a singular verb. Choice (C) is incorrect because the *-ing* form is not a verb, and a clause requires a verb. Choice (D) is incorrect because the verb is active, and a passive verb is needed.

In the Written Expression section, verb errors often involve the following:

1. *A main verb may be used instead of a participle or vice versa.* The main verb, for example *eat* or *ate,* may be used instead of *eaten,* or the main verb *is eating* instead of *eating.*

2. *The gerund may be used instead of the infinitive.* For example, *eating* instead of *to eat.*

3. *The wrong infinitive form may be used.* For example, *make* may be used instead of *to make.*

4. *The wrong form of the participle may be used.* The present participle may be used instead of the past participle or vice versa.

   Example: In the 1931 Winter Olympics, many <u>competitors</u> were
   A
   <u>prevented</u> from <u>to participate</u> <u>because of</u> the economic
   B   C   D
   depression.

   The best answer is (C). An infinitive cannot be used after a preposition. The gerund form *participating* must be used.

EXERCISES ON VERBS   Answers on page 187

> **Choose the one word or phrase that best completes the sentence.**

1. The first systematic chart ever made of an ocean current _____ by Benjamin Franklin.

   (A) published
   (B) was published
   (C) publishing
   (D) has been published

2. Petroleum _____ on every continent and beneath every ocean.

   (A) is found
   (B) found
   (C) are found
   (D) find

3. Animals _____ on Earth for at least 700 million years.

   (A) living
   (B) lived
   (C) have lived
   (D) have been lived

4. During the Ice Age, glaciers _____ and retreated several times over large areas of the earth.

   (A) had been advanced
   (B) were advanced
   (C) have advanced
   (D) advanced

5. Some fish _____ distortions of electrical fields through special receptors.

   (A) sense
   (B) are sensing
   (C) are sensed
   (D) senses

6. The widespread use of oil and gas to make chemicals _____ during the 1920s.

   (A) has begun
   (B) began
   (C) beginning
   (D) begun

> **Choose the one underlined word or phrase that must be changed for the sentence to be correct.**

7. The American architect, Frank Lloyd Wright, <u>developed</u> a theory of
                                                     A

   architecture <u>stressed</u> the needs of the people <u>who</u> <u>used</u> it.
              B   C   D

8. Pelicans <u>have</u> a long, straight bill with a <u>flexible</u> pouch <u>makes</u> of skin on
           A   B   C

   the <u>underside</u>.
        D

9. In some countries, octopuses and snails <u>are considered</u> <u>being</u> great
                                           A   B

   <u>delicacies</u> <u>to</u> eat.
       C   D

10. Many dyslexics <u>have</u> difficulty <u>to remembering</u> the <u>sequence</u> of letters in
                   A   B   C

    a word and in <u>distinguishing</u> right from left.
                  D

11. Men and women in the Peace Corps <u>work</u> with people in <u>developing</u>
                                     A   B

    countries to help them <u>improving</u> their <u>living</u> conditions.
                           C   D

12. Seahorses <u>spend</u> <u>much</u> of their time <u>clung</u> with their tails to <u>underwater</u>
                A   B   C   D

    plants.

CHAPTER 5 PREPOSITIONS

Introduction: Mount St. Helens

Mount St. Helens, a volcano in the state of Washington in the United States, erupted on May 18, 1980. Sixty-two people died due to the eruption. No one was surprised by the eruption on Mount St. Helens. Scientists had been predicting that an eruption was likely for almost two years before it happened.

In March 1980 a small eruption occurred, and in April one side of the mountain started to swell and crack. The scientists issued warnings and asked people to clear the area. On May 18 the mountain exploded. Hot gases burst out, followed by hot ash, which ran down the mountain slopes burning everything in its path. Two cubic kilometers of earth was thrown 60,000 feet straight up into the atmosphere. Cities and towns were covered with powder. The ash from the volcano was found as far away as the Atlantic Ocean, on the other side of the continent.

The top of the mountain was blown away and about 600 square kilometers (230 miles) of land was destroyed, killing both animals and plants. Many thought it would take decades for the land to recover, but the return of life was remarkable. Today the slopes and valleys of Mount St. Helens once again have abundant wildlife.

EXERCISE 1   Answers on page 187

> **Prepositions are tested on the TOEFL® test. Complete the sentences with the correct prepositions.**

1. Mount St. Helens erupted _____ May 18, 1980.
2. Scientists had predicted that an eruption was likely, so no one was surprised _____ it.
3. _____ April 1980 one side _____ the mountain started to swell.
4. The explosion of hot gases was followed _____ hot ash.
5. Cities were covered _____ ash from the mountain.
6. The ash _____ the mountain went as far as the Atlantic Ocean _____ the other side of the continent.

CHAPTER 5   PREPOSITIONS   49

EXERCISE 2   Answers on page 187

Look at the chart below showing natural disasters. Describe the disaster, including when it occurred, where it occurred, and what happened due to the disaster. The first one is done for you.

Disaster	Where	When	What Happened
1. Volcanic eruption	Krakatoa, Indonesia	August 27, 1883	36,000 people died
2. Potato famine	Ireland	1840s	1.5 million people died
3. Flood	Johnstown, Pennsylvania, U.S.	May 1889	2200 people died
4. Earthquake	Tangshan, China	July 28, 1976	242,000 people died
5. Tidal wave	Bangladesh	1970	200,000 people died
6. Tornado	Ohio, U.S.	April 3, 1974	315 people died
7. Fire	Yellowstone Park, U.S.	1980	1.3 million acres burned

1. *A volcanic eruption **occurred in** Krakatoa **on** August 27, 1883. **Due to** the eruption, 36,000 people died.*

Grammar: Prepositions

Prepositions are not only used to show time, place, and agent but are also used in combination with verbs, adjectives, nouns, and in many common set expressions. This chapter cannot list all prepositions, but it will present the important groups:

1. Verb + Preposition

   depend on   lead to

2. Adjective/Participle + Preposition

   surprised at   famous for

3. Noun + Preposition

   example of   possibility of

4. Other Combinations with Prepositions

   as a result of   in addition to

5. Prepositions of Time and Place

   on May 16   in Washington

6. Prepositions in Common Expressions

   at present   in general

Peterson's ■ In-A-Flash: Grammar for the TOEFL   www.petersons.com

> **Strategy**
>
> Since the use of prepositions and their rules can be very confusing for many learners of English, it is best to learn as many prepositions as possible in combination with other words. Errors on the exam may include the wrong preposition being used or a preposition being omitted where it should not be.

VERB + PREPOSITION

account for	contribute to	insist on	plan on
believe in	depend on	lead to	rely on
belong to	detach from	obtain from	result in
confined to	fight for	overcome by	withdraw from

EXERCISE 3   Answers on page 188

> **Complete the sentences with the correct prepositions.**

1. The destructive phenomena of Mount St. Helens were not confined _____ volcanic debris.

2. Valuable chemical products are obtained _____ volcanic substances, including gold and silver.

3. The 1989 San Francisco earthquake resulted _____ 59 deaths and massive property damage.

4. One growing season after another without rain quickly leads _____ starvation in many parts of the world.

5. Disease can sometimes be overcome _____ advances in modern medicine.

6. Since the Irish depended _____ their potato crop for food, the potato famine had devastating results.

7. Poor farming practices contributed _____ the dust bowl as much as weather conditions.

8. When there is famine in a country, the people must rely _____ the goodwill of other countries to provide them with the food they need.

ADJECTIVE/PARTICIPLE + PREPOSITION

accustomed to	different from	necessary for	responsible for
afraid of	expert at	opposed to	successful in
based on	free from	possible for	surprised at
compared to	famous for	related to	typical of

EXERCISE 4   Answers on page 188

Complete the sentences with the correct prepositions.

1. The 1980 Mount St. Helens eruption ranks low compared _____ other volcanic eruptions.

2. Some people think it is necessary _____ forest fires to happen occasionally so that new trees will grow.

3. Typical _____ American enterprise, a thriving cottage industry developed in marketing the ash from Mount St. Helens.

4. Volcanic ash in the atmosphere is responsible _____ brilliant red sunsets and sunrises.

5. The earth looks very different _____ the way it looked millions of years ago.

6. The type of gas ejected from a volcanic eruption is related _____ the volcano and the type of eruption.

7. Countries whose economy is entirely based _____ agriculture suffer most when a crop fails.

8. People were surprised _____ the amount of destruction the eruption of Mount St. Helens caused.

NOUN + PREPOSITION

cause of	equivalent of	influence on	result of
cost of	evidence of	need for	use of
danger of	example of	possibility of	solution to
effect on	increase in	reason for	supply of

EXERCISE 5   Answers on page 188

Complete the sentences with the correct prepositions.

1. Mount St. Helens exploded in an eruption with the energy equivalent _____ 10 million tons of TNT.

2. With the ever-growing need _____ power, volcanoes and their by-products are of increasing value.

3. To the scientist, volcanoes provide first-hand evidence _____ the composition of the earth.

4. An example _____ an island that consists entirely of volcanic material is Iceland.

5. Iceland, Italy, New Zealand, and the state of California make practical use _____ volcanic steam.

6. The El Chichon eruption in Mexico had the greatest effect _____ the world's weather.

7. In recent years, the crater of Vesuvius has been sealed off to lessen the danger _____ another explosion.

8. Plague and famine can be results _____ social problems within a community.

OTHER COMBINATIONS WITH PREPOSITIONS

according to	in the process of
as a consequence of	in view of
as a result of	on account of
because of	on behalf of
by means of	on the basis of
in addition to	prior to
in spite of	with the exception of
in terms of	with the purpose of

EXERCISE 6   Answers on page 188

> **Complete the sentences with the correct prepositions.**

1. According _____ some reports, the effect of the tsunami from Krakatoa was felt 11,000 miles away.

2. In addition _____ seismographs, tilt meters measure deformations of the surface before volcanic activity.

3. The loss in terms _____ individual trees after the Mount St. Helens eruptions came to six million.

4. Airplanes and trains were affected because _____ poor visibility after the eruption.

5. In view _____ their devastating results, much thought has been given to forecasting volcanic eruptions.

6. Thirty-five people died as a result _____ the Mount St. Helens eruption.

7. In spite _____ the death and destruction volcanoes cause, they benefit the land in many ways.

8. Prior _____ the eruption, a 300-foot bulge was observed on one side of Mount St. Helens.

PREPOSITIONS OF TIME AND PLACE

* Prepositions of Time

at	time of day (at 8 a.m.)
	noon, night, midnight
in	parts of the day (in the morning/evening/ afternoon)
	month (in July)
	season (in the fall)
	year (in 1980)
	decade (in the 1980s)
	century (in the nineteenth century)
on	days of the week (on Monday)
	dates (on March 20)
for/since	duration of time (for three days)
	point in time (since March 20)
from . . . to	from beginning time . . . to ending (from 8 a.m. to 5 p.m.)

• Prepositions of Place

at	address (at 200 Main Street)
on	street/road/avenue (on Kings Road)
	floor (on the second floor)
in	building (in the drugstore)
	city (in Los Angeles)
	state (in California)
	country (in Japan)
	continent (in Africa)
from . . . to	from beginning point . . . to ending point (from Alaska to California)

EXERCISE 7   Answers on page 188

Complete the sentences with the correct prepositions.

1. Mount St. Helens had last erupted _____ 1857.

2. Mount St. Helens exploded _____ about 8 a.m. _____ Sunday.

3. The eruption was _____ May 18, 1980.

4. _____ the summer of 1816, the weather _____ the United States was affected by volcanic activity.

5. Mount St. Helens is _____ the state of Washington.

6. The volcano Paricutin _____ Mexico erupted _____ 1943.

7. Before the eruption, Mount St. Helens was one of the most beautiful areas _____ North America.

8. Most houses _____ Reykjavik _____ Iceland are heated by natural steam.

9. Mount St. Helens was active _____ March 20 _____ May 18, 1980.

10. A chain of volcanoes runs _____ the East Indies _____ the Mediterranean.

PREPOSITIONS IN COMMON EXPRESSIONS

at times	by land/sea/air	in common	on fire
at present	by far	in general	on the other hand
at first/last	by chance	in existence	on the whole
at the moment	by accident	in the future/past	on purpose
	by day/night	in theory	on land

EXERCISE 8   Answers on page 188

Complete the sentences with the correct prepositions.

1. Volcanoes _____ land are best known, but those beneath the sea sometimes make headline news.

2. _____ times volcanoes have affected world weather.

3. _____ theory, volcanic eruptions are difficult to classify.

4. There are about 500 volcanoes _____ existence.

5. It looked as if the mountain were _____ fire.

6. Volcanic ash is destructive; _____ the other hand, it later produces very fertile soil.

7. _____ general, a temperature of 100°C is reached at about 10,000 feet in the earth's crust.

8. Mount St. Helens was _____ far the most publicized eruption in recent times.

On the TOEFL® Test

Prepositions are tested in the Written Expression section of the exam. Check for the following two types of errors with prepositions.

1. The wrong preposition is used.

   Example: Mount St. Helens, <u>a</u> volcano <u>in Washington state</u>
                     A   B
   <u>in the United States</u>, <u>erupted in May 18</u>, 1980.
         C   D

   The best answer is (C). The preposition *on* must be used before a date (*in* is used before a month without a date).

   Example: <u>After the eruption</u> of Mount St. Helens <u>in 1980</u>, the <u>height of</u>
           A   B   C
   the mountain was <u>reduced of</u> 400 meters.
                   D

   The best answer is (D). The preposition *by* should be used after the verb "reduce" in this sentence.

2. A preposition may be omitted or a preposition may be used when it is not necessary.

Example: <u>Despite of</u> its isolation <u>in the Sunda Strait</u> between Java and
         A   B   C

                 Sumatra, over 36,000 people died <u>in the tidal waves</u> follow-
                                             D

                 ing the explosion of Krakatoa.

The best answer is (A). The preposition *of* should not be used in this phrase (*of* is used in the phrase *in spite of,* but *despite,* which has the same meaning, does not take a preposition).

Example: <u>According experts,</u> 60,000 <u>cubic feet of earth</u> was thrown
                  A   B

                 <u>into the air</u> <u>in the explosion of</u> Mount St. Helens.
                   C   D

The best answer is (A). The preposition *to* has been omitted from the phrase *according to.*

EXERCISES ON PREPOSITIONS   Answers on page 188

> **Choose the one underlined word or phrase that must be changed for the sentence to be correct.**

1. The rocky island of Alcatraz <u>in San Francisco Bay</u> was <u>discovered by</u> the
                               A   B

   Spanish <u>in 1769</u> and <u>named by</u> its large pelican colony.
            C   D

2. Bacteria are <u>responsible of</u> <u>many of the textures</u> and flavors <u>in our food</u>
               A   B   C

   and are particularly <u>important in</u> milk products.
                       D

3. Art Nouveau, a style that was <u>in fashion</u> <u>in the 1890s,</u> was <u>based of</u> long
                            A   B   C

   curving lines <u>inspired by</u> climbing plants.
              D

4. The brain is <u>made up of</u> <u>billions of neurons</u> that <u>differ with</u> each other
               A   B   C

   greatly <u>in size and shape.</u>
              D

5. Wood, the hardened <u>material from which</u> trees are <u>composed,</u> is
                   A   B

   <u>made up of millions</u> <u>of tiny tubes of fibers</u> packed together.
           C   D

6. Animals that <u>live in areas</u> that are <u>covered in</u> snow <u>in winter</u> change the
                        A   B   C
color of their coat <u>according</u> the seasons.
                         D

7. The need for <u>vitamins of our diet</u> was <u>discovered by</u> the Dutch doctor
                  A   B   C
Christiaan Eijkman <u>in 1896</u>.
                        D

8. <u>Many of the satellites</u> <u>of space</u> carry telescopes and other instruments
                 A   B
<u>used in astronomy</u> to <u>look at the stars</u>.
         C   D

9. Homes that have cable television <u>get their programs</u>
                                              A
<u>from a local television station</u> <u>through a cable</u> <u>connected with</u> the set.
                 B   C   D

10. Henry David Thoreau stressed <u>the importance in</u> individuality and
                                          A
<u>of living</u> <u>in harmony</u> <u>with nature</u>.
     B   C   D

11. The hormone insulin <u>controls by</u> the amount <u>of sugar</u> <u>in the blood</u>,
                              A   B   C
which <u>provides energy</u> for the body.
            D

12. Frogs get <u>much of their</u> oxygen <u>by means blood</u> capillaries <u>in the surface</u>
                    A   B   C
<u>of the skin</u>.
     D

ARTICLES

Introduction: Islands

The world's ten largest islands (drawn to scale)

Island	Ocean		Island	Ocean
1. Greenland	Arctic		6. Sumatra	Indian
2. New Guinea	Pacific		7. Honshu	Pacific
3. Borneo	Pacific		8. Great Britain	Atlantic
4. Madagascar	Indian		9. Victoria	Arctic
5. Baffin Island	Arctic		10. Ellesmere	Arctic

Borneo

New Guinea

Madagascar

Greenland

Baffin
Island
(Canada)

Honshu
(Japan)

Great Britain

Sumatra

0   500 km

Victoria (Canada)

Ellesmere
(Canada)

Some islands were originally parts of continents. These islands were separated from the mainland as a result of a rise in sea level. For example, Great Britain was connected to the mainland of Europe about 11,000 years ago. As the climate got warmer, ice melted and the sea level rose. As a result, water covered the land that had connected Great Britain to the mainland.

Other islands rise from the ocean. Some are volcanoes, such as the islands of Hawaii and the islands of Japan. Some volcanic islands are millions of years old, but new islands are forming all the time. For example, Iceland was formed millions of years ago by a volcano, but as recently as 1963, a volcano started to form a new island called Surtsey near Iceland.

Islands differ greatly in size. Greenland is the largest island in the world. The difference between an island and a continent is based on size. Because Australia is three times the size of Greenland, geographers classify Australia as a continent.

EXERCISE 1   Answers on page 188

Articles are tested on the TOEFL® test. Complete the sentences with the name of the country or island.

1. Honshu is the biggest island in _____.

2. _____ is the biggest island in the world.

3. According to geographers, _____ is not an island but a continent.

4. About 11,000 years ago _____ was connected to Europe.

5. _____ was formed by a volcano millions of years ago.

6. _____ is a new island formed in 1963.

EXERCISE 2   Answers on page 188

Complete the sentences below with information from the chart on page 58.

1. Greenland is the largest island. It is in the _____ Ocean.

2. _____ is the second largest island. It is in the _____ Ocean.

3. _____ is _____ third largest island. It is in _____ _____ Ocean.

4. _____ is _____ _____ largest island. It is in _____ _____ Ocean.

5. _____ is _____ fifth largest island. It is in _____ _____ Ocean.

6. _____ is _____ _____ largest island. It is in _____ _____ Ocean.

Grammar: Articles

THE INDEFINITE ARTICLE A OR AN

Strategy

Avoid confusion between *a* and *an*. Remember, *an* is used before a vowel sound.

There are a number of rules for using the indefinite articles *a* or *an*.

- Use *a* or *an* before singular count nouns to mean *one*. The indefinite article is not used before noncount nouns.

  Australia is a continent.

- Use *an* before a word that begins with a vowel sound (a, e, i, o, u). When words begin with "h" or "u," either *a* or *an* can be used depending on the sound:

an uncle	*a home*
a university	*an hour*
a union	*an honor*

- Use *a* or *an* in a general statement:

An island is a body of land surrounded by water.

- Use *a* or *an* to introduce a subject that has not been mentioned before:

I saw a snake.

- Use *a* or *an* with certain numerical expressions:

a dozen	*a couple*	*a hundred*	*a third*	*a half*
a great many	*a great deal*	*a lot of*	**fifty miles*	**$10 a day*
			an hour	

* In this case *a/an* is a replacement for *per*.

- Use *a* or *an* with names of professions:

He is an engineer.   She is a biologist.

EXERCISE 3   Answers on page 188

Circle *a* or *an* in the following sentences. Write "C" on the left if the sentence is correct. Write "NC" if the sentence is not correct and correct the error.

_____ 1. Indonesia is a country made up of thousands of islands.

_____ 2. Greenland is an big island with a permanent ice cap covering it.

_____ 3. The Bahamas, which consist of 700 islands, have a superb climate.

_____ 4. Robinson Crusoe is a character in a book by Daniel Defoe.

_____ 5. Robinson Crusoe spent twenty years with his friend Man Friday on a uninhabited island.

_____ 6. New Guinea is a country where there are a large number of languages.

_____ 7. Etna is an active volcano on the island of Sicily.

_____ 8. On the island of Borneo, there is a snake that can fly or leap up to 20 meters.

_____ 9. The plants and an animals that live on an island may develop to be quite different.

THE DEFINITE ARTICLE *THE*

The definite article *the* can be used before any noun, singular, plural, count, and noncount, when the noun is specific.

> *the* island
> *the* islands
> *the* water

There are a number of ways to use the definite article.

1. When there is only *one* of the thing mentioned:

   The sun is shining.
   The sky is blue.

2. When it is clear to both the speaker and the listener which thing or person is referred to:

   *Could you open **the** door please?* (Both the speaker and the listener know which door it is.)

3. Before a noun mentioned for the second time:

   *A bird flew into the classroom. **The** bird sat on my desk.*

4. Before superlative adjectives:

   The biggest island is Greenland.
   The most beautiful coral island is very small.

5. Before names of musical instruments:

   *He plays **the** piano.*

6. Before a singular noun representative of a class of things (names of animals, plants, inventions, and parts of the body):

   The dodo is an extinct bird.
   The Rafflesia is the world's largest flower.
   *Alexander Graham Bell invented **the** telephone.*
   *He hit me on **the** head.*

Strategy

Remember the uses of the definite article. On the exam, it may be omitted when it should not be.

7. Before decades and centuries:

   the 1800s   *the twenties*   *the twentieth century*

8. Before expressions of time and place:

the morning	*the future*
the afternoon	*the present*
the evening	*the past*

the north	*the front*
the south	*the back*
the east	*the middle*
the west	*the top*
	the bottom

9. Before ordinal numbers (the definite article is not used with cardinal numbers):

Ordinal numbers:	Cardinal numbers:
the first	one
the second day	day two
the sixth lesson	lesson six

10. When speaking about a specific noun:

    Coffee originated in Ethiopia. (general)
    The coffee I had this morning was Brazilian. (specific)

11. Before names of countries, states, cities, universities, colleges, and schools that contain the word *of*, and before countries that have a plural name or have an adjective in the name, except for Great Britain:

    the United States of America
    the state of Florida
    the city of Boston
    the University of Texas
    the Netherlands
    the Philippines
    But: *Boston University*

12. Before names of oceans, rivers, seas, gulfs, and plural names of mountains, islands, and lakes (no article is used with singular mountains, islands, and lakes):

the Pacific Ocean   *the Mississippi River*
the Gulf of Mexico   *the Black Sea*
the Appalachian Mountains   But: *Mount Washington*
the Hawaiian islands   But: *Manhattan Island*
the Great Lakes   But: *Lake Michigan*

13. Before geographic areas, but not before names of continents:

the Middle East   But: *Asia*
the Orient   *Europe*

14. Before the names of fields of study when they contain the word *of:*

the History of the United States   But: *history*
the Literature of the Sixties   *biology*

15. Before the names of wars (not including the World Wars):

the War of Independence   *the Civil War*
But: *World War II*   *the Second World War*

16. Before the names of ships, planes, trains, and people's family names (the definite article is not used with the names of people and names of magazines):

the Browns   But: *Robert Brown*
the Mayflower   Time *Magazine*
the Orient Express

EXERCISE 4   Answers on page 188

> **Fill in the blanks with the correct article *a, an, the,* or ø if no article is needed.**

1. Islands make up _____ entire land area of some countries, including _____ Japan and _____ Philippines.

2. _____ Florida Keys are coastal islands built on coral reefs.

3. _____ Mackinac Island in _____ Lake Michigan is _____ lake island.

4. _____ city of Montreal, in _____ Canada, is built on _____ large river island.

5. _____ Aleutian Islands, part of _____ Alaska, are _____ string of coastal islands that were built by _____ volcanoes.

6. On _____ big island of Hawaii is one of _____ world's greatest volcanoes, _____ Mauna Loa.

7. Kilauea is _____ most active volcano in _____ state of _____ Hawaii.

8. The early settlers of _____ Pacific Islands, _____ Polynesians, always carried _____ coconuts with them in their canoes.

9. In _____ Indonesia is _____ huge lizard, _____ Komodo Dragon, that eats deer and attacks people.

10. _____ dodo, a giant bird now extinct, lived on _____ island of Mauritius, in _____ Indian Ocean.

On the TOEFL® Test

Articles are tested in the Written Expression section of the exam. Check for the following three types of errors with articles.

1. The article may be used when it is not necessary, or not used when it is necessary.

   Example: Pelican Island in Florida and Oregon Islands in Oregon are
   A   B   C
   wildlife refuges.
   D

   The best answer is (C). The definite article *the* should not be omitted from the name of a plural group of islands.

   Example: The most coral islands develop from reefs that grow up
   A   B   C
   around volcanic islands.
   D

   The best answer is (A). This is not a superlative form; therefore the article is not necessary.

2. *An* is used instead of *a* or vice versa. Also *a* or *an* may be used instead of *the* or vice versa.

   Example: A broad expanse of sea with a large number of islands is
   A   B   C
   called a archipelago.
   D

   The best answer is (D). *An* must be used before a noun beginning with a vowel sound.

Example: When <u>the island</u> of <u>Surtsey</u> was eighteen months old, <u>a first</u>
     A   B   C

    <u>leafy green plant</u> appeared.
       D

The best answer is (C). The definite article *the* must be used with an
ordinal number.

3. Another word, like a possessive adjective, may be used instead of the
article (or vice versa.)

   Example: <u>The new</u> island <u>of Surtsey</u> is <u>its ideal</u> natural laboratory
        A   B   C

     <u>for scientists</u>.
       D

The best answer is (C). The indefinite article *an* meaning "one" must be
used.

   Example: <u>Coral reefs</u> are <u>limestone formations</u> composed of
         A   B

     <u>tiny sea organisms</u> and <u>the remains</u>.
        C   D

The best answer is (D). The possessive adjective *their* must replace the
definite article *the* to show its reference to sea organisms.

Exercises on Articles   Answers on page 189

> **Choose the one underlined word or phrase that must be
> changed for the sentence to be correct.**

1. The <u>watt</u> is named after James Watt, <u>the British</u> engineer who developed
    A   B

  <u>the steam engine</u> in <u>1760s</u>.
     C   D

2. <u>Methane</u> is <u>a odorless</u> burning gas and is <u>the main</u> ingredient of
   A   B   C

  <u>natural gas</u>.
    D

3. <u>The alcohol</u> acts as a <u>narcotic</u> on <u>the nervous system</u> and <u>the brain</u>.
    A   B   C   D

4. Zachary Taylor was <u>first president</u> to be elected from <u>a state</u> <u>west</u> of
          A   B   C

  <u>the Mississippi River</u>.
     D

5. Barnacles, which are related to lobsters, shrimp, and crabs, make
       A   B   C
   strongest glue.
       D

6. In the 1860s, Louis Pasteur discovered that bacteria in air caused
         A   B
   the perishable food to go bad.
           C   D

7. Land covers almost third of the earth's surface, of which two thirds is
     A   B   C   D
   too cold or too dry for farming.

8. "Old Faithful" in the Yellowstone National Park is probably the world's
          A   B   C
   most famous geyser.
       D

9. Thermographs are special pictures that show the variation in heat
     A   B   C
   emitted by different areas of body.
                    D

10. The world's fastest animal is cheetah, but if birds are included,
        A   B
    the fastest of all animals is the spine-tailed swift.
      C   D

11. The most of the energy used in our homes and factories is generated
        A   B
    from coal, oil, and natural gas.
        C   D

12. Soybeans were first grown in the Orient and brought to the Western
      A   B   C
    world during the World War Two.
            D

CHAPTER 7
NOUN CLAUSES

Introduction: Michael Faraday

During the last 400 years, most scientists have relied on mathematics in their development of their inventions or discoveries. However, one great British scientist, Michael Faraday, did not make use of mathematics. Faraday, the son of a poor blacksmith, was born in London in 1791 and had no education beyond reading and writing.

In 1812, Faraday was hired as a bottle washer by the great chemist Humphry Davy. Later, Faraday became a greater scientist than Davy, making the last years of Davy's life embittered with jealousy.

In 1821, Faraday made the first electric motor, a device that used electricity to produce movement. Then Faraday became interested in the relationship between electricity and magnetism. In 1831 he discovered that when a magnet is moved near a wire, electricity flows in the wire. With this discovery he produced a machine for making electricity called a dynamo. Faraday then went on to show how electricity affects chemical substances.

Because Faraday believed that money should be given to the poor, when he grew old, he was destitute. However, Queen Victoria rewarded him for his discoveries by giving him a stipend and a house. He died in 1867.

EXERCISE 1   Answers on page 189

> **Noun clauses are tested on the TOEFL® test. Complete the blanks in the following sentences with *that* and *how*.**

1. Humphry Davy was jealous _____ Faraday became a greater scientist than he.

2. Faraday discovered _____ when a magnet is moved near a wire it produces electricity.

3. Faraday showed _____ electricity affects chemical substances.

4. Faraday showed _____ great scientific discoveries could be made without the use of mathematics.

5. Faraday believed _____ money should be given to the poor.

6. Faraday's invention meant _____ homes could be heated by electric power and lit by electric light.

EXERCISE 2   Answers on page 189

Choose the correct noun clause to complete the sentence.

1. Faraday discovered _____.
   (A) that a magnet creates electricity in a wire
   (B) what electricity is

2. Faraday showed _____.
   (A) why electricity does not affect chemicals
   (B) how electricity affects chemical substances

3. It was obvious _____.
   (A) why Humphry Davy was jealous of Faraday
   (B) how Humphry Davy was jealous of Faraday

4. Faraday believed _____.
   (A) what everybody told him
   (B) that money was not important

5. It can be seen _____.
   (A) how mathematics is important to scientific discovery
   (B) that mathematics is not necessarily important in scientific discovery

Grammar: Noun Clauses

A noun clause is a subordinate clause. A noun clause has a subject and a verb and can be used like a noun, either as a subject or an object.

- As subject

  His discovery was important.
     Noun

  His discovery is a noun. It is the subject of the sentence.

  What he discovered was important.
     Noun clause

  What he discovered is a noun clause. It is the subject of the sentence. It has a subject *he* and a verb *discovered*.

* As object

> *People believed <u>his discovery</u>.*
>   Noun

His discovery is a noun. It is the object of the verb *believed*.

> *People believed <u>what he discovered</u>.*
>   Noun clause

What he discovered is a noun clause. It is the object of the verb *believed*.

Noun clauses are introduced by the following words:

when	who/whom	whether	that
where	what	if	
why	which		
how	whose		

NOUN CLAUSES BEGINNING WITH A QUESTION WORD

Question words such as *when, where, why, how, who/whom, what, which*, and *whose* can introduce a noun clause.

	Question	Noun Clause
1.	What did he discover?	I don't know *what he discovered.*
2.	When did he discover it?	I'm not sure *when he discovered it.*
3.	Where did he discover it?	It is not known *where he discovered it.*
4.	How did he discover it?	I'm not certain *how he discovered it.*
5.	Who is Faraday?	I don't know *who he is.*
6.	Whose discovery is that?	It is not certain *whose discovery that is.*
7.	What did he discover?	*What he discovered* is not certain. (*What he discovered* is the subject of the sentence.)

> **Strategy**
>
> Do not use question word order in a noun clause. The subject comes before the verb in a noun clause.

EXERCISE 3   Answers on page 189

> **Which of the following sentences do not have correct word order in the noun clause? Write "C" for correct or "NC" for not correct.**

_____ **1.** It is amazing what discovered Faraday in the field of science without the use of mathematics.

_____ **2.** Early scientists did not know how a strong, steady electrical current could be produced.

_____ **3.** How Faraday did his experiments without the use of mathematics is not known.

_____ **4.** In the early 1800s it was unknown what was the electric current.

_____ **5.** People have known what are the effects of electricity since ancient times.

_____ **6.** Before Faraday's experiments, people were unsure what the connection between electricity and magnetism was.

NOUN CLAUSES BEGINNING WITH *WHETHER* OR *IF*

When a yes/no question is changed to a noun clause, *whether* or *if* is used to introduce the clause.

Question	Noun Clause
Will it work?	He wonders *whether it will work.*
	He wonders *if it will work.*
Did they believe him?	I don't know *whether they believed him.*
	I don't know *if they believed him.*

NOUN CLAUSES BEGINNING WITH *THAT*

For a statement of a fact or an idea, the word *that* is used to introduce the noun clause.

	Statement	Noun Clause
1.	The world is round.	We know *that the world is round. (That the world is round* is the object of the verb *know*.)
2.	The world is round.	We know *the world is round.* (The word *that* is frequently omitted in spoken English.)
3.	The world is round.	*That the world is round* is a fact. (*That the world is round* is the subject of the sentence. The word *that* cannot be omitted when it introduces a noun clause that is the subject of a sentence.)

Strategy

A noun clause must have a subject and a verb. Look for a subject and a verb when the noun clause is the object or the subject of a sentence.

EXERCISE 4   Answers on page 189

Choose the one word or phrase that best completes the sentence.

1. Faraday argued that _____.
   - (A) electricity in a wire magnetic effect
   - (B) electricity in a wire by magnetic effect
   - (C) electricity in a wire produced a magnetic effect
   - (D) a magnetic effect produced by electricity in a wire

2. It is a fact that _____ form of energy.
   - (A) electricity is the most useful
   - (B) electricity the most useful
   - (C) the most useful in electricity
   - (D) electricity being the most useful

3. _____ over long distances is a fact.
   - (A) That electricity can be transmitted
   - (B) That electricity transmitting
   - (C) That electricity
   - (D) That can be transmitted

4. Today it is known that _____ magnetism.
   - (A) electricity relating to
   - (B) electricity is related to
   - (C) relating to electricity
   - (D) as electricity to

5. _____ in science was important for Faraday.

(A) Children that were interested
(B) That children interested
(C) That children should be interested
(D) That interested children

6. After listening to Humphry Davy, Faraday realized that _____.

(A) wanting to be a scientist
(B) being a scientist
(C) wanted to be a scientist
(D) he wanted to be a scientist

On the TOEFL® Test

In a typical noun clause error, a part of the noun clause is missing from the stem. The missing part may be the introductory word, the subject, the verb, or even the whole noun clause.
    It is important to:

1. Look for the correct word order in the distractors.

2. See if the noun clause has a subject and a verb.

3. Find the correct introductory word for the noun clause.

   Example: _____ was flat was believed by most people in the fifteenth century.

(A) The Earth
(B) That the Earth
(C) As the Earth
(D) Whether the Earth

The best answer is (B). Choice (A) is not correct because there are two verbs—_was_ and _was believed_—and only one subject. Choice (C) is incorrect because the introductory word does not make sense in the sentence. Choice (D) is incorrect because it does not have a subject.

   Example: Many scientists have shown _____ can be used for an ever-increasing number of tasks.

(A) that lasers how
(B) lasers how
(C) how lasers
(D) that what lasers

The best answer is (C).

EXERCISES ON NOUN CLAUSES   Answers on page 189

Choose the one word or phrase that best completes the sentence.

1. Astronomers studied the 1987 Supernova to learn _____ when a star explodes.

   (A) what happens
   (B) that happens
   (C) that is happen
   (D) what does happen

2. Despite recent attempts to prove _____ did indeed reach the North Pole in 1909, the evidence still remains questionable.

   (A) what Robert Peary
   (B) that Robert Peary
   (C) Robert Peary, who
   (D) Robert Peary was

3. Around 1789, Antoine Lavoisier was the first person to demonstrate _____ all kinds of burning involve the addition of oxygen.

   (A) if
   (B) what
   (C) that
   (D) so that

4. Where _____ is the commonest form of color-blindness.

   (A) are the red and green not easily distinguished
   (B) they are not easily distinguished red and green
   (C) are not easily distinguished red and green
   (D) red and green are not easily distinguished

5. It has been estimated _____ milligram of skin scales has over half a million bacteria.

   (A) that a
   (B) how a
   (C) a
   (D) to be a

6. It is only in the last 200 years _____ have begun climbing mountains.

   (A) because people
   (B) that people
   (C) people
   (D) as people

7. _____ of smell might, without our realizing it, affect who we choose as friends has been suggested.

   (A) That our sense
   (B) Sense
   (C) For our sense
   (D) Because our sense

8. From the existence of radio waves, most scientists were convinced _____ really happened.

(A) the Big Bang was
(B) it was the Big Bang
(C) how the Big Bang
(D) that the Big Bang

9. Samples of rock showed _____ 4600 million years old.

(A) that the moon is
(B) how is the moon
(C) when is the moon
(D) to be the moon

10. _____ was lowered to the sea bed in a glass container to make observations is debated.

(A) Alexander the Great who
(B) Whether or not Alexander the Great
(C) Alexander the Great
(D) What Alexander the Great

11. _____ so incredible is that it can grow 385 miles of roots in four months, or about 3 miles in a day.

(A) That makes the rye plant
(B) What makes the rye plant
(C) The rye plant
(D) The rye plant which was

12. Science fiction writers believe _____ in the future, with new material and greater knowledge, their visions will become reality.

(A) that they
(B) they
(C) that
(D) they will

ADJECTIVE CLAUSES

Introduction: American Indian Smoke Signals

The smoke signals used by American Indians did not convey the complex messages seen in Hollywood movies. Smoke signals were in fact used among the seminomadic tribes of the Great Plains. However, their content was limited to a few simple messages whose meaning had been agreed upon in advance. For example, Piman warriors in Arizona who had just finished a successful raid might send up a column of smoke, and the village would reply with two columns of smoke. Smoke signals were most commonly used to broadcast news of victory in battle, or to warn of sickness in a camp or dangers such as approaching enemies.

Fires fed with damp grass or boughs of evergreen sent up the one or two simple, unbroken columns of smoke needed to send a message. The place that the signal came from—whether on a hill or in a valley—conveyed most of the meaning. When Apaches out hunting spotted another group of Indians in the distance, they lit a fire conspicuously to the right of their own party that meant, "Who are you?" If the others were friends, they would then use a prearranged reply.

EXERCISE 1   Answers on page 189

> **Adjective clauses are tested on the TOEFL® test. Complete the sentences with the relative pronouns *which, who, whose, that*.**

1. Smoke signals, _____ the American Indians used, did not convey complex messages.

2. The signals contained simple messages _____ meaning had been agreed upon in advance.

3. A warrior _____ had finished a successful raid might send a simple column of smoke to his village.

4. They made fires, _____ were then fed with damp grass.

5. It was the place the signal came from _____ conveyed most of the message.

6. When one group spotted another group of Indians, they lit a fire to their right, _____ meant, "Who are you?"

EXERCISE 2   Answers on page 189

Choose the correct relative pronoun in parentheses to complete the sentence.

1. The seminomadic tribes of the Great Plains used smoke signals, (which/ who) were simple.

2. A signal (whose/which) conveyed victory in battle was agreed upon in advance.

3. The Hollywood movies (that/whom) we watch do not give a true picture of the Indians.

4. A party would send a column of smoke, (which/whom) the other party understood.

5. Drumbeats, (whose/which) are used by tribes in Africa, can give more complex signals.

6. A warrior (who/which) saw an enemy approaching might send a smoke signal.

Grammar: Adjective Clauses

An adjective clause contains a subject and a verb. An adjective clause is a subordinate or dependent clause, so it must be connected to a main or independent clause. An adjective clause modifies a noun. Adjective clauses begin with a relative pronoun such as *who, whom, whose, which, that,* or a relative adverb such as *when* or *where.*

IDENTIFYING ADJECTIVE CLAUSES

Clause Marker	Use	Example
who	People (subject)	The tribes *who* lived in the Great Plains used smoke signals.
whom	People (object)	The woman *whom* we met was called Lightning Cloud.
whose	People/things (possessive)	He sent a message *whose* meaning we had agreed upon in advance.
which	Things (subject/object)	That is a tribe *which* interests me. (subject)
		The drumbeats *which* we heard sent a message. (object)
that	People/things (subject/object)	The Apache is a tribe *that* I will research. (object)
		The smoke *that* you see is from the hills. (subject)
where	Place (adverb)	That is the valley *where* the tribe lived.
when	Time (adverb)	That is the day *when* we get the signal.

Strategy

Check for the correct clause marker and a subject and verb in an adjective clause.

EXERCISE 3   Answers on page 189

Underline the adjective clauses in the following sentences.

1. Sacagawea, who was a Shoshoni Indian, guided Lewis and Clark to the Columbia River.

2. The giant redwood trees that grow in California are named after Sequoyah, who created an alphabet for the Indian people.

3. Sequoyah became a teacher and moved to Oklahoma where he continued to teach the alphabet.

4. The Shoshoni were a group of Indians who lived in the western plains of Wyoming, Utah, Nevada, and Idaho.

5. Each group of Shoshoni was known to the others by the type of food that was plentiful in its particular region.

6. The Mossi people of West Africa use talking drums as a means of preserving their history, which has been handed down by generations.

Strategy

Remember that sometimes the relative pronoun may be omitted from an adjective clause. The relative pronouns *which, that, who,* and *whom* can be omitted when they are the object of the adjective clause.

OMISSION OF THE RELATIVE PRONOUN

When the relative pronoun is the subject of the adjective clause, it cannot be omitted.

> *The man **who** played the drum was from West Africa.* (subject)

If the relative pronoun is the object of the adjective clause, it can be omitted.

> *The man **whom** I saw was a Native American.* (object)
> *The man I saw was a Native American.*

> *The drumbeat **that** I heard was a signal.* (object)
> *The drumbeat I heard was a signal.*

The relative pronouns *whose, where,* and *whereby* cannot be omitted.

> *Sequoyah, **whose** alphabet for the Indian people consisted of 85 characters, was acclaimed a genius by his people. (Whose* cannot be omitted.)

> *That was the area **where** the tribe lived. (Where* cannot be omitted.)

> *Sequoyah devised an alphabet **whereby** all the different tribes could read a common language. (Whereby* cannot be omitted.)

Strategy

Look for prepositions that come before adjective clauses.

PREPOSITIONS THAT COME BEFORE ADJECTIVE CLAUSES

Sometimes an adjective clause is used with a preposition.

*There are a number of ways **by which** a message can be sent.*

In spoken English the preposition usually goes at the end of the clause, but in formal written English it goes at the beginning of the clause.

Formal: *That was the man **to whom** I was referring.*
Informal: *That was the man **whom** I was referring **to.***

EXERCISE 4   Answers on page 189

Circle the number of the sentence where the relative pronoun/adverb or a preposition is missing.

1. Lewis and Clark went to South Dakota, where they spent a bitter winter among the Mandan tribe.

2. It is countries such as Ghana, Dahoney, and Nigeria the use of talking drums is mostly highly developed.

3. The most celebrated talking drummers of West Africa are the Yorubas, whose principal instrument is known as a dondon.

4. Talking drums, play a central role in African cultural and social life, have many uses besides the sending of long-distance messages.

5. There are a number of colors which the Pueblo Indians of America identified direction.

6. Drumbeats which the actual words of their tribal language is communicated is a traditional form of communication in Africa.

> **Strategy**
>
> Look for a reduced adjective clause, also called an adjective phrase. An adjective phrase does not contain a subject and a verb.

REDUCED ADJECTIVE CLAUSES

Adjective clauses can be reduced to phrases. An adjective phrase modifies a noun. An adjective phrase does not contain a subject and a verb.

Adjective Clause: *The man who is drumming is African.*
Adjective Phrase: *The man drumming is African.*

Only adjectives that have a subject pronoun, *who, which,* or *that,* can be reduced.

Clause: *The man who is playing the drums is well-known.*
Phrase: *The man playing the drums is well-known.*

Clause: *The man (whom) I met was well-known.*
Phrase: *not possible*

There are two ways to reduce an adjective phrase.

1. The subject pronoun and the *be* form of the verb are omitted.

   Clause: *The man who is playing is my friend.*
   Phrase: *The man playing is my friend.*

   Clause: *The signals which are given are simple.*
   Phrase: *The signals given are simple.*

   Clause: *The tones that are in the language are important.*
   Phrase: *The tones in the language are important.*

2. When there is no form of *be* in the adjective clause, you can omit the subject pronoun and change the verb to the *-ing* form.

   Clause: *The Cherokee Indians have an alphabet that consists of eighty-five characters.*
   Phrase: *The Cherokee Indians have an alphabet consisting of eighty-five characters.*

   Clause: *Anyone who wants to get the news can listen to the message.*
   Phrase: *Anyone wanting to get the news can listen to the message.*

   Adjective phrases are usually separated by commas, as in adjective clauses.

   Clause: *Sequoyah, who was the inventor of an Indian alphabet, was a Cherokee Indian.*
   Phrase: *Sequoyah, the inventor of an Indian alphabet, was a Cherokee Indian.*

EXERCISE 5   Answers on page 189

> **Where possible, reduce the adjective clauses to phrases.**

1. Sequoyah, who was the son of an Indian mother and a European father, was born in Tennessee.

2. Sequoyah, who was first a hunter, became a trader after a hunting accident.

3. Sequoyah, who had no education, believed that reading and writing were important.

4. Sequoyah, who worked on the alphabet for twelve years, finally completed it in 1823.

5. His alphabet, which consists of eighty-five sounds, was an important invention for his people.

6. A Cherokee newspaper whose columns had news both in English and Cherokee was soon published.

7. Thousands of Cherokees who did not know how to read or write started to write using the new alphabet.

On the TOEFL® Test

> Adjective clauses are tested in the Structure section of the exam. In the item, certain or all parts of an adjective clause may be missing. It is important to remember what an adjective clause is and what an adjective phrase is, that is, if a subject and verb are necessary or not.

Example: Pythons live in rugged tropical areas _____ heavy rainfall and forests.

(A) they have
(B) that have
(C) where the
(D) have

The best answer is (B). Choice (C) is incorrect because *where* is the incorrect connector and the clause does not have a verb. Choice (A) is incorrect because there is no connector joining the first and second clause. Choice (D) is incorrect because there is no connector between the verb *have* and the rest of the sentence.

Reduced adjective clauses are also tested in the Structure section. Again, part or all of the phrase may be missing from the stem.

Example: In 1880, George Eastman, _____ dry-plate manufacturer, introduced the Kodak box camera.

(A) who an American
(B) he was an American
(C) an American
(D) was an American

The best answer is (C). Choice (A) is incorrect because there is no verb in the relative clause. Choice (B) does not have a connector to join the clause to the rest of the sentence. Choice (D) is not correct because it contains a verb, and a phrase cannot have a verb.

EXERCISES ON ADJECTIVE CLAUSES   Answers on page 190

> **Choose the one word or phrase that best completes the sentence.**

1. The thyroid gland, _____, is located in the neck.

    (A) where the hormone thyroxine is produced
    (B) where produced is the hormone thyroxine
    (C) the hormone thyroxine is produced there
    (D) at which is produced the hormone thyroxine

2. Dragonflies feed on a large variety of insects, _____ catch in flight.

    (A) in which they
    (B) which they
    (C) there are to
    (D) there are a

3. According to legend, Betsy Ross was the woman _____ the first American stars and stripes flag.

    (A) whom she made
    (B) made
    (C) who made
    (D) and she made

4. Pumpkin seeds, _____ protein and iron, are a popular snack.

    (A) that
    (B) provide
    (C) which
    (D) which provide

5. The spinal cord is a long, thick bundle of nerves _____ from the brain to the lower part of the back.

    (A) that runs
    (B) is running
    (C) it runs
    (D) whom it runs

6. George Pullman introduced a dining car _____ its own kitchen in 1868.

    (A) it had
    (B) that had
    (C) that it had
    (D) having

7. In 1898, _____ pharmacologist, John H. Abel, isolated the hormone adrenaline.

    (A) an American who
    (B) who, an American
    (C) an American
    (D) he was an American

8. Nitrogen gas, _____ up about 78 percent of our atmosphere, is constantly being used by plants and animals.

    (A) which it makes
    (B) it makes
    (C) makes
    (D) which makes

9. Paper is made from cellulose fibers, _____ in all cells.

    (A) are
    (B) which are
    (C) they are
    (D) which they are

10. The pepper plant bears a small, green berry, _____ red as it ripens.

    (A) which turns
    (B) turns
    (C) it turns
    (D) that it turns

11. Quinine, _____ once used to cure malaria, was taken from the bark of a South American tree, the cinchona.

    (A) it is a famous drug
    (B) is a famous drug
    (C) a famous drug
    (D) is a famous drug whose

12. Billie Holiday, _____ unique singing style made her famous, was also known as Lady Day.

    (A) she is a
    (B) whom
    (C) who
    (D) whose

CHAPTER 9 · ADVERB CLAUSES

Introduction: Distant Galaxies

The development of the radio telescope has led to two of the most important discoveries in modern astronomy: the identification of the most distant galaxies and the smallest stars ever seen. Before these discoveries were made, new large telescopes had to be built.

The most distant galaxies are called quasars. They were discovered in 1963 when astronomers noticed strong radio signals coming from small points in the sky. When the radio astronomer Maarten Schmidt from Mount Palomar Observatory looked at these points, he saw faint galaxies that could be seen only because they were shining brightly. These galaxies, or quasars, were the most powerful objects ever discovered and are the most distant objects ever seen. Some are over 13,000 million light-years away. They get their power from a huge black hole at their center.

A black hole is a region of space where the pull of gravity is so strong that even light cannot escape. When gas and dust fall into the black hole at the center of a quasar, they produce large amounts of light and heat. Although black holes are very small, they are extremely heavy. A black hole less than a centimeter across can weigh the same amount as the Earth. The black holes in the center of quasars may weigh up to 100 million times as much as our sun.

EXERCISE 1   Answers on page 190

> **Adverb clauses are tested on the TOEFL® test. The blanks in the sentences introduce adverb clauses. Complete the blanks with one of the following words: before, when, because, although.**

1. New, large telescopes had to be built _____ important discoveries were made.

2. Quasars were discovered _____ astronomers noticed radio signals.

---

3. Maarten Schmidt saw faint galaxies _____ he looked at points in the sky.

4. The points could be seen _____ they shone brightly.

5. Light and heat are produced in the center of a quasar _____ gas and dust fall into it.

6. _____ black holes are small, they are extremely heavy.

EXERCISE 2   Answers on page 190

> ### Choose the correct adverb clause marker from the parentheses.

1. Quasars are an important discovery (because/although) they are the most powerful objects ever seen.

2. The outer planets are cooler than the inner ones (as/whereas) they are further from the sun.

3. A black hole is a region of space (where/whenever) the gravitational pull is so strong that nothing can escape.

4. Radio waves from distant regions of space could be studied (while/after) the radio telescope was invented.

5. Telescopes see distant objects more clearly (whereas/because) radio telescopes collect radio waves.

6. Astronomers did not know about quasars (before/so that) radio telescopes were invented.

Grammar: Adverb Clauses

An adverb clause is a subordinate clause (dependent clause) with a subject and a verb. An adverb clause may come before or after the main clause (independent clause). When it comes before the main clause or at the beginning, it is usually separated from the main clause by a comma.

> ***When** Schmidt looked at the small points, he saw galaxies.*
> *Schmidt saw galaxies **when** he looked at the small points.*

ADVERB CLAUSE MARKERS

The following are some common words used to introduce an adverb clause.

- Clause markers showing time:

after	by the time	until
as	once	when
before	since	whenever
as soon as	till	while

  *Meteors glow **as** they burn up in the atmosphere.*
  *It was difficult to observe the stars **before** the telescope was invented.*

- Clause markers showing manner:

  as   as if   as though   just as   like

  *Ancient peoples used the stars **as if** they were calendars.*
  *The Milky Way looks **as though** it is a faint band of light.*

- Clause markers showing cause and effect:

because	since	as
now that	as long as	so that

  *Spacesuits were designed for astronauts **so that** they could breathe in space.*
  ***Since** some planets are too far away to send people, computer-operated space probes are sent.*

- Clause markers showing opposition:

although	while
though	whereas
even though	

  *Most stars are white **while** some are colored.*
  ***Although** helium is rare on Earth, it is common in the universe.*

- Clause markers showing condition:

if	in the event that	provided that	unless
even if	in case that		
only if			

  *You will see hundreds of stars **if** you look at the sky.*
  *You can study distant stars **provided that** you have a radio telescope.*

- Clause markers showing purpose:

    so that   in order that   so (that)
               in order to   (*That* is often omitted in
                                  spoken English.)

    *Astronomers improved telescopes **so that** they would discover more
        about the stars.*
    *Astronomers developed bigger and bigger telescopes **in order to** see
        the stars more clearly.*

- Clause markers showing result:

    so . . . that   such . . . that

    *The stars are **so** far away **that** they cannot be seen without a telescope.*
    *The meteor hit the Earth with **such** force **that** it made a crater.*

- Clause markers showing place:

    where   wherever   everywhere

    *There were stars **wherever** she looked.*
    *A crater was formed **where** the meteor hit the earth.*

Strategy

Look for the adverb clause markers and make sure that the adverb clause
has both a *subject* and a *verb*.

EXERCISE 3   Answers on page 190

Underline the adverb clauses in the following sentences.

1. Although millions of meteors hit the earth's atmosphere, few of them
   are noticed.

2. A meteor leaves a bright trail as it streaks across the night sky.

3. Many meteorite falls are not noticed because they hit the earth in
   remote uninhabited areas.

4. The rate of the sun's radiation is so great that about 3 million tons of
   matter is converted into energy every second.

5. In ancient times, farmers planted crops when they saw a planet in the
   right part of the sky.

6. Even though a planet moves among the stars, it returns to the same part
   of the sky at the same time each year.

REDUCED ADVERB CLAUSES

Adverb clauses may be reduced to modifying phrases in the same way as adjective clauses are reduced to modifying phrases. A reduced adverb clause or modifying phrase does not contain a subject or a verb. It consists of a participle (present or past participle) or an adjective and clause marker (*although, when,* or *while*).

Full: ***After*** *the space probes landed on Mars, they sent back pictures.*
Reduced: ***After landing on Mars, the space probes sent back pictures.***

Full: ***Although*** *the moon rocks were expensive to obtain, they provided valuable information.*
Reduced: ***Although*** *expensive to obtain, the moon rocks provided valuable information.*

An adverb clause may be changed to a modifying phrase only when the subject of the main clause and the adverb clause are the same.

Adverb clause: ***After*** *the space probe landed on Venus, it mapped the surface.*
Modifying phrase: ***After*** *landing on Venus, it mapped the surface.*

Adverb clause: ***After*** *the space probe sent pictures, astronomers examined them.*
Modifying phrase: *not possible*

PREPOSITIONAL EXPRESSIONS

Some prepositions have almost the same meaning as some of the clause markers, but they can be used only with nouns, noun phrases, or pronouns. They cannot be used with clauses.

Strategy

The following prepositions cannot be used in clauses: *because of, on account of, in case of, in spite of, despite, during.* When you see them, look for nouns, noun phrases, or pronouns in the distractors.

Cause/effect: *Many of the planets are cratered **because of** meteor bombardment.*

Concession: ***In spite of** the damage to the spacecraft, the astronauts got back to Earth safely.*

Condition: ***In case of** contamination, special suits were worn.*

Time: *Radio receivers were used **during** the Second World War.*

EXERCISE 4   Answers on page 190

> **The following sentences contain adverb clauses, reduced adverb clauses, and prepositional expressions. Choose the one word or phrase that best completes the sentence.**

1. _____ the ancient Chinese and Egyptians took astronomy seriously, the Greeks were the first to study the stars scientifically.

   (A) Although
   (B) Despite
   (C) For
   (D) Nevertheless

2. _____ the development of radio telescopes, distant regions of the Universe can be observed.

   (A) The reason
   (B) Because of
   (C) Because
   (D) It is because

3. Supernovas are caused _____ a star dies.

   (A) as when
   (B) that
   (C) when
   (D) it is

4. In 1987 a Canadian astronomer, Ian Shelton, spotted a supernova _____ looking at some photographs of the stars.

   (A) was
   (B) during
   (C) as if
   (D) while he was

5. _____ the 1987 supernova was so near, astronomers were able to study it carefully.

   (A) Although
   (B) Since
   (C) It was
   (D) As it was

6. _____ used simple instruments, the ancient Greek astronomer, Hipparchus, made the first accurate map of the stars 2100 years ago.

   (A) Even though
   (B) Even though he
   (C) Nevertheless
   (D) In spite of

On the TOEFL® Test

Adverb clauses are tested in the Structure part of the exam. In these items, any part of the adverb clause may be missing from the stem; it may be the clause marker, the subject, the verb, or other parts of the clause.
It is important to remember the following:

1. An adverb clause contains a subject and a verb.

2. A reduced adverb clause does not contain a subject and a verb.

3. Use the correct clause marker for the adverb clause.

   Example:_____ the solar system may seem big, it is a very small part of the universe.
   (A) Despite
   (B) Although
   (C) Even though it
   (D) Because

   The best answer is (B). Choice (A) is incorrect because *despite* cannot be used in an adverb clause that has a subject and a verb. Choice (C) is incorrect because it contains a subject, *it*, which is repeated again in the same clause. Choice (D) is incorrect because it contains the wrong clause marker, giving reason instead of concession.

   Example: Ancient astronomers looked at the stars _____ could make predictions about the future.
   (A) they
   (B) so
   (C) so that they
   (D) as they

   The best answer is (C).

EXERCISES ON ADVERB CLAUSES   Answers on page 190

Choose the one word or phrase that best completes the sentence.

1. Plexiglas is used in aircraft windows _____ is almost unbreakable.

   (A) it
   (B) because it
   (C) because
   (D) it because

2. American Indians grew popcorn for a few thousand years _____ arrival of European explorers in the 1400s.

   (A) before
   (B) before the
   (C) since
   (D) since they

3. The body uses proteins for energy _____ and fats cannot meet its energy needs.

   (A) that carbohydrates
   (B) when carbohydrates
   (C) when they are carbohydrates
   (D) that when carbohydrates

4. Spider monkeys are the best climbers in the jungle, _____ they do not have thumbs.

   (A) nevertheless
   (B) for
   (C) despite
   (D) although

5. Stars are hot bodies that give out light of their own, _____ planets shine only by reflecting light.

   (A) however there are
   (B) since
   (C) whereas
   (D) while they

6. A silkworm has glands that secrete a liquid that hardens into silk _____ comes into contact with air.

   (A) as it
   (B) when
   (C) that
   (D) it

7. _____ their immense distances, quasars have relatively high magnitudes.

   (A) Whereas
   (B) In spite of
   (C) Although
   (D) Yet

8. _____ body's activities put strains on certain bones, these bones strengthen themselves where the stress is greatest.

   (A) That if
   (B) That
   (C) Because of
   (D) If the

9. _____ Herman Melville is now regarded as one of America's finest writers, his greatest works mystified readers in his own lifetime.

(A) It is despite
(B) Despite
(C) Even though
(D) In spite of

10. _____ laser beam can be moved easily in all directions, it can be used for highly accurate cutting in industry.

(A) Because of
(B) It is a
(C) A
(D) As a

11. Limestone powder is added to animal feed _____ animals form good strong bones.

(A) why
(B) so that
(C) as a result of
(D) it is that

12. _____ sodium chloride (salt) is not used by sea-living organisms, it forms the dominant mineral in seawater.

(A) Since
(B) It is since
(C) Although
(D) Although it

CHAPTER 10

PREPOSITIONAL PHRASES

Introduction: Land Art

The land art movement first appeared in the U.S. in the late 1960s. Most of the work was created in a landscape setting, using whatever materials the artist came across. Part of its appeal was that in many cases the artist's work was quickly changed by the forces of nature. For example, Robert Smithson built a vast spiral jetty from earth and stones in the Great Salt Lake in Utah. Now deposits of salt and sulphur have completely changed the way it looks.

Some land artists welcomed such impermanence, because it meant their work could not be owned. As land art was often in wild, out-of-the-way places, it was rarely seen by the public. Many artists therefore recorded their activities in words, photographs, and so on.

Richard Long is one of the most famous and successful land artists. Much of his work consists of going for long, carefully planned walks in wild and lonely parts of the world. Sometimes he leaves his mark by making small changes to the landscape, such as forming a line of stones. More recently he has brought back objects from his walks and used them to make up sculptures in art galleries.

EXERCISE 1   Answers on page 190

> **Prepositional phrases are tested on the TOEFL® test. Fill in the blanks with the correct preposition in the prepositional phrase.**

1. It was _____ the 1960s _____ the United States that an art movement called land art started.

2. Land art is created _____ a landscape setting _____ wild parts _____ the world.

3. Many times the artist's work is changed _____ nature.

4. Robert Smithson built a jetty _____ earth and stone _____ the Great Salt Lake _____ Utah.

5. Land art is found _____ out-of-reach places and is therefore not seen _____ many people.

6. Land artists often record their work _____ text or photographs.

EXERCISE 2   Answers on page 190

Correct the prepositions in the following sentences.

1. Richard Long leaves his mark by making changes with the landscape.

2. Richard Long brings back found objects of his walks.

3. Richard Long uses the objects in sculptures that are shown on art galleries.

4. Land art involves the artist going into nature, usually from a remote area.

5. The only record that remains of land art is photographic, sometimes combined of maps.

Grammar: Prepositional Phrases

The following are some common prepositions:

about	behind	in	through
above	below	in spite of	throughout
across	beneath	into	till
after	beside	like/unlike	to
against	between	near	toward
along	beyond	of	under
among	by	off	until
around	despite	on	up
as	down	out	upon
at	during	out of	with
because of	for	over	within
before	from	since	without

A prepositional phrase consists of a preposition and an object. The object may be a noun or a pronoun.

The work	*is changed*	*by*	*nature* .
subject	verb	preposition	object of preposition

The work	*is changed*	*by*	*it* .
subject	verb	preposition	object of preposition

The noun may have modifiers. In this case it is called a noun phrase.

Land art	*is*	*in*	*wild*	*places* .
subject	verb	preposition	modifier	object of preposition

EXERCISE 3   Answers on page 190

Mark the subject S, verb V, object O, and prepositional phrases PP in the following sentences.

1. Artists have painted nature for centuries.

2. Richard Long recorded his work in different ways.

3. Most murals are painted in a naturalistic style.

4. The role of art in Western culture has changed in the last hundred years.

5. Futurism emerged in northern Italy before the First World War.

6. Some contemporary artists have rejected art galleries for political reasons.

Strategy

Look for the preposition and its object. Some words used as prepositions may not be used in a prepositional phrase.

Do not confuse a clause with a prepositional phrase.

> Not a prepositional phrase: ***Because** it changed, the work was impermanent.*

> Prepositional phrase: ***Because of** change, the work was impermanent.*

In other cases, a phrasal verb may cause confusion. A phrasal verb is a verb with one or two prepositions that together have a special meaning.

> Not a prepositional phrase: *The artist **ran across** an old sketch.*
> (The phrasal verb "run across" means to meet by accident.)

> Prepositional phrase: *The artist ran **across** the room to get a canvas.*

EXERCISE 4   Answers on page 191

Underline the prepositional phrases in the following sentences.

1. The invention of photography in the 1820s encouraged artists to attempt even greater realism in their paintings.

2. As the nineteenth century wore on, some artists began to question the need for art to refer to the outside world.

3. By the nineteenth century, art dealers had begun to sell uncommissioned art to a wider public.

4. Monet was more concerned with expressing an almost mystical sense of communion with nature than with working spontaneously.

5. With the Industrial Revolution, the landscape began to change more and more, and artists began to look into its negative and positive aspects.

6. Land art involves the artist going out into nature, usually in a remote area, and making his or her mark on it.

Strategy

Make sure you choose the correct preposition. To review prepositions, see Chapter 5.

EXERCISE 5   Answers on page 191

Choose the preposition that best completes the sentence.

1. Artists have painted nature _____ centuries.

   (A) for
   (B) in
   (C) since
   (D) by

2. As Europe became more industrialized, art began to reflect a growing nostalgia _____ the old rural way of life.

   (A) in
   (B) for
   (C) of
   (D) to

3. By the twentieth century, artists were becoming less conventional _____ the way they portrayed landscape and nature in general.
   - (A) by
   - (B) as
   - (C) in
   - (D) for

4. Cubism was the result _____ a gradual process of change.
   - (A) on
   - (B) with
   - (C) in
   - (D) of

5. _____ with landscape, seventeenth century Dutch artists were the first to paint still lifes for their own sake.
   - (A) As
   - (B) In
   - (C) Since
   - (D) Beyond

6. The key role of the still life in modern art has been as a focus _____ technical and stylistic experiments.
   - (A) in
   - (B) on
   - (C) with
   - (D) to

7. Futurists were inspired _____ the dynamism of the machine age.
   - (A) with
   - (B) of
   - (C) by
   - (D) on

8. Op art became a very trendy movement and had a big influence _____ fashion.
   - (A) in
   - (B) to
   - (C) with
   - (D) on

On the TOEFL® Test

Prepositional phrases often appear at the beginning of a sentence but may also appear in other parts of the sentence. The wrong preposition will appear in the distractors, or a clause may be used in the distractors without a connector to join it to the other clause.

It is important to remember that the subject of a sentence cannot be the object of a preposition.

Example: _____ turn of the century, the first art galleries and museums were built.
   - (A) The
   - (B) Around the
   - (C) It was around the
   - (D) When the

The best answer is (B). Choice (A) is not correct as there is no connector joining the noun phrase "the turn of the century" with the rest of the sentence. Choice (C) is a clause, but there is no connector joining it to the other clause. Choice (D) looks like a subordinate clause but does not have a verb.

Example: _____ realistic painting or sculpture, emotion is expressed mainly through people's poses and expression.

(A) In a
(B) It is in a
(C) As
(D) A

The best answer is (A). Choice (B) is a clause but there is no connector joining it to the other clause. Choice (C) looks like a clause but does not have a verb. Choice (D) is not correct as there is no connector joining it to the rest of the sentence.

EXERCISES ON PREPOSITIONAL PHRASES Answers on page 191

From the four words or phrases, choose the _one_ that best completes the sentence.

1. Camels store water _____ of fat in their humps.
   (A) with the form
   (B) in the form
   (C) by the form
   (D) form

2. Tears contain an antiseptic that helps protect our eyes _____ infection.
   (A) from bacterial
   (B) in bacterial
   (C) bacterial
   (D) with bacterial

3. So far only two other of our neighboring planets _____ the solar system have been visited by unmanned spacecraft.
   (A) by
   (B) that they are in
   (C) in
   (D) they are by

4. Many tropical orchids grow _____ branches of trees and have aerial roots that absorb water from the moist air around them.
   (A) of the
   (B) the
   (C) they are in the
   (D) in the

5. _____ compact disc, sound is stored as digital information in tiny pits on the surface.

   (A) On a
   (B) A
   (C) It is on a
   (D) Of a

6. Giraffes sleep only _____ an hour at a time and often do not sleep at all during twenty-four hours.

   (A) by
   (B) for
   (C) in
   (D) during

7. _____ were invented, patients had to be held down by force during painful operations.

   (A) As anesthetics
   (B) Because anesthetics
   (C) Before anesthetics
   (D) Anesthetics

8. The surface of a cactus is coated _____ waxy layer that prevents water from evaporating from the plant.

   (A) it is a
   (B) a
   (C) by a
   (D) with a

9. _____ eighteenth century, people began to realize that certain chemicals are affected and changed by light.

   (A) By the
   (B) The
   (C) It was the
   (D) That in the

10. In addition to their homes, the Pomo Indians of California built dance houses _____ religious ceremonies.

    (A) of
    (B) for
    (C) in which
    (D) were for

11. The wood of many pine species makes excellent pulp _____ manu-
    facture of paper.

    (A) in
    (B) to
    (C) for the
    (D) the

12. The photos of the American Civil War made by Matthew Brady and his
    assistants rank _____ finest war pictures of all time.

    (A) the
    (B) in the
    (C) between the
    (D) among the

COMPARATIVES AND SUPERLATIVES

Introduction: Violins

| Violin | Viola | Cello | Double Bass |

For many years the violin was looked down on as a lesser musical instrument; music was not composed especially for it except in overtures to court pageants or background music for aristocratic drawing rooms. However, beginning around 1680 into the nineteenth century, a succession of Italian violinist composers created an enormous amount of music for the violin—people such as Corelli, Vivaldi, Pugnani, Paganini, and Viotti.

The violin is the principal member of the violin family. The other members are the viola, the cello, and the double bass. The full-size violin, which is the smallest and highest pitched of the stringed instruments played with a bow, has a body size of fourteen inches. The viola is slightly larger than the violin, and it has a slightly richer but less brilliant tone. It is really an alto violin, and it fills the gap between the violin and the cello.

The greatest of the violin makers was Antonio Stradivari, who was born in 1644. During his lifetime, Stradivari made over a thousand stringed instruments, of which about six hundred are still in existence.

EXERCISE 1   Answers on page 191

> **Comparatives and superlatives are tested on the TOEFL® test. Complete the sentences with the comparative or superlative form from the reading.**

1. People looked down on the violin as a _____ musical instrument.

2. The violin is the _____ and _____ pitched of the stringed instruments played with a bow.

3. The viola is _____ than the violin.

4. The viola has a _____ tone than the violin.

5. But the viola has a less _____ tone than the violin.

6. Antonio Stradivari was the _____ violin maker.

EXERCISE 2   Answers on page 191

> **Fill in the blanks with one of the following words:**
> **small   big   smaller   bigger   biggest   smallest**

1. The double bass is the _____ of the violin family.

2. The cello is _____ than the double bass.

3. The cello is _____ than the viola.

4. The viola is not as _____ as the cello.

5. The violin is not as _____ as the viola.

6. The violin is the _____ of the violin family.

Grammar: Comparatives and Superlatives

THE COMPARATIVE AND SUPERLATIVE OF ADJECTIVES

There are three forms of comparison: the absolute (the base form of the adjective), the comparative, and the superlative.

1. The absolute form is used to describe a thing or person.

   *The violin is a **small** instrument.*

2. The comparative is used when comparing two things, or when comparing something(s) with other things.

   *The violin is **smaller than** the cello.*

3. The superlative is used when comparing more than two things, or when one in a group has the greatest amount of a quality.

   *The violin is **the smallest** of the violin family.*

Strategy

Check to see that the correct form of the comparative and superlative is used where needed on the TOEFL® test.

---

a. The comparative and the superlative of one-syllable adjectives are formed by adding *-er* and *-est* to the absolute.

Absolute	Comparative	Superlative
small	smaller	smallest
high	higher	highest

b. The comparative and the superlative of adjectives of three or more syllables are formed by adding *more* and *most*.

Absolute	Comparative	Superlative
brilliant	more brilliant	most brilliant
important	more important	most important

> **Strategy**
>
> Check to see that the absolute, comparative, and superlative structures are formed correctly in TOEFL® test questions.

c. Some adjectives ending in -*er, -y,* or -*le* form comparatives and superlatives by adding -*er* or -*est* to the absolute form ("y" changes to "i").

Absolute	Comparative	Superlative
early	earlier	earliest
simple	simpler	simplest

THE COMPARATIVE AND SUPERLATIVE OF ADVERBS

The forms used for the comparison of adjectives are also used for the comparison of adverbs.

d. For the comparative and superlative forms of all one-syllable adverbs use -*er* and -*est*.

Absolute	Comparative	Superlative
fast	faster	fastest
quick	quicker	quickest

e. For all other adverbs use *more* and *most.*

Absolute	Comparative	Superlative
slowly	more slowly	most slowly
commonly	more commonly	most commonly

f. The following are irregular comparatives and superlatives of adjectives and adverbs.

Absolute	Comparative	Superlative
good (adj)	better	best
well (adv)	better	best
bad (adj)	worse	worst
badly (adv)	worse	worst
little (adj/adv)	less	least
many (adj)	more	most
much (adj/adv)	more	most
far (adj/adv)	farther	farthest
	further	furthest
late (adv)	later	last
old (adj)	older	oldest
	elder	eldest

g. The comparative form *less* and the superlative form *least* are used with both adjectives and adverbs to show that something does not have as much as something else.

*This mass-produced violin is **less** expensive.*

*Of the mass-produced violins, this one is the **least** expensive.*

OTHER FORMS OF THE COMPARATIVE

- *As . . . as / Not as . . . as / Not so . . . as*

    When things that are equal are compared, the following forms can be used:

    as . . . as
    not as (positive) as
    not so (positive) as

    *There are not **as** many violin makers today **as** there were in the past.*

    *Playing the violin is **not as** difficult **as** you might think.*

- *The Double Comparative*

    The double comparative is used to show parallel increase or decrease.

    the + comparative . . . *the* + comparative

    ***The more** he plays, **the more** he improves.*
    ***The shorter** the string, **the higher** the note.*

- *As and Like*

    In a simple comparison, *like* is used before a noun or pronoun.

    *You play the cello with a bow **like** the violin.*

    If a verb follows the noun and pronoun, *as* must be used.

    *You play the cello with a bow **as** you do the violin.*

EXERCISE 3   Answers on page 191

> **Underline the comparatives that are incorrect in the following sentences.**

1. Stretching a string more tightly gives a highest note.

2. The violin is probably the most importantest of all orchestral instruments.

3. The viols are bowed strings that are more older than the violin family.

4. The viols do not have as bright a sound the violin family.

5. The heavier the string, the low the note it sounds.

6. Small violins have short strings than full-sized instruments, but they play the same notes.

7. Andres Segovia is the more famous classical guitarist in the world.

On the TOEFL® Test

> In the Structure section, adjectives are usually compared. The forms *as . . . as, the more . . . the more, similar to, different from, unlike,* and so on may appear in this section.

Example: _____ tilted toward the sun, the more heat it receives and the hotter it is.

(A)   As more as the earth is
(B)   The more the earth is
(C)   The earth is more than
(D)   The earth is most

The best answer is (B). It should have the construction *the more . . . the more.*

In the Written Expression section, the three forms of the comparative and superlative (the absolute, comparative, or superlative) may be used incorrectly.

Example: The Great Plains region of the United States <u>suffered</u> one of
                                                                          A
the <u>worse</u> <u>droughts</u> <u>in history</u> from 1931 to 1938.
        B   C   D

The best answer is (B). The sentence does not compare two groups, and therefore, the superlative *worst* is required.

EXERCISES ON COMPARATIVES AND SUPERLATIVES

Answers on page 191

> **Choose the one word or phrase that best completes the sentence.**

1. Temperature, the simplest weather element to measure, is probably _____ used than any other kind of data.

   (A) more frequently
   (B) most frequently
   (C) as frequently
   (D) frequently

2. Paprika is _____ red or cayenne pepper, and it has a sweeter taste.

   (A) least biting
   (B) less biting than
   (C) lesser biting than
   (D) less as

3. The foods that contain _____ are made of animal fat whereas vegetables have the least energy.

   (A) as much energy as
   (B) the more energy
   (C) the most energy
   (D) more energy than

4. Albert Einstein's contributions to scientific theory were _____ those of Galileo and Newton.

   (A) important than
   (B) more important
   (C) the most important
   (D) as important as

5. Impalas cannot move as _____ cheetahs, but they are more efficient runners.

   (A) faster than
   (B) fast as
   (C) fast
   (D) are fast as

6. Apart from Pluto, the outer planets _____ the inner planets and are made mainly of lighter materials such as hydrogen and helium.

   (A) are larger than
   (B) are the largest
   (C) larger than
   (D) are large

> ## Choose the one underlined word or phrase that must be changed for the sentence to be correct.

7. During the 1700s, Philadelphia <u>developed</u> into the <u>most wealthy</u> city in
     A   B   C
   the <u>American</u> colonies.
        D

8. <u>According to</u> Freud, the mind <u>experiences</u> more <u>unconsciouser</u> than
      A   B   C
   <u>conscious</u> activity.
     D

9. Eleanor Roosevelt <u>was</u> one of the <u>most activest</u> and <u>influential</u> <u>first</u>
               A   B   C   D
   ladies.

10. The Sahara Desert in Africa is <u>by far</u> the <u>most large</u> desert in the world,
                             A   B
   covering an area <u>nearly</u> <u>as big as</u> the United States.
               C   D

11. Peanuts are <u>closely</u> <u>related</u> <u>to</u> peas than <u>to</u> nuts.
      A   B   C   D

12. Most evergreens have <u>needle-like</u> leaves that require <u>least</u> water than
      A   B   C
   <u>regular</u> leaves.
     D

CHAPTER 12 CONJUNCTIONS

Introduction: The Soya Bean's Industrial Uses

Soya is not only used in the manufacture of food for human and animal consumption but also in a variety of industrial processes. These range from the manufacture of adhesives and plastics to dynamite and waterproofing preparations.

For many years soya bean oil has been used in the manufacture of paints, both for domestic and industrial use. It is also used in the printing industry in printing inks, adhesives, and paper. In the United States the soya bean is used in the brewing industry to help the yeast ferment and enhance the flavor of beer.

Soya is even used in fire-fighting as a foam agent. When mixed with water and air it produces the fire-fighting foam. Water might put out the surface flames, but the fire could still be burning underneath. Fire-fighting foam on the other hand clings to most surfaces and does not drain as quickly as water. If oil has caught fire, the foam floats on the surface and smothers the flames.

Glycerine, which is a byproduct of vegetable oils including soya, is used in nearly every industry. It is an ingredient in many medicines including cough mixtures and is also a basic medium in toothpaste. Glycerine is not only used in glues to prevent quick drying, but also in the manufacture of explosives. No doubt as research and experiments continue, even more uses for this versatile crop will be found.

EXERCISE 1   Answers on page 191

> **Conjunctions are tested on the TOEFL® test. Fill in the blanks with one of the following conjunctions: *and, but,* or *or.***

1. Soya is used in the printing industry in printing inks, adhesives, _____ paper.

2. In the brewing industry soya helps the yeast to ferment _____ enhances the flavor of the beer.

3. When soya is mixed with water _____ air it produces a fire-fighting foam.

4. Water might put out the flames _____ the fire would still be burning underneath.

5. Fire-fighting foam clings to surfaces _____ does not drain as quickly as water.

6. Glycerine is used in many medicines including cough mixtures _____ is the basic medium in toothpaste.

EXERCISE 2   Answers on page 192

> **Correct the mistakes with the following constructions in the sentences: *not only . . . but also* or *both . . . and.***

1. Soya is used not only in many food processes and also in many industrial processes.

2. Soya has been used in the manufacture of paints for both industrial or domestic use.

3. Glycerine is used not only in glues but in the manufacture of explosives.

4. Soya is used in the manufacture of food for both human consumption but also animal consumption.

5. American farmers have been encouraged to grow more soya not only because the export market has expanded also because the demand at home has increased.

6. The ancient Chinese used the soya bean for both food and also medicine.

Grammar: Conjunctions

Conjunctions are tested in both the Structure and Written Expression sections. The two kinds of conjunctions tested are:

a. Coordinating conjunctions

b. Correlative conjunctions

COORDINATING CONJUNCTIONS

Coordinating conjunctions connect words or phrases that have the same function in a sentence. The coordinating conjunctions tested on the TOEFL® test are *and, but, or,* and *so.*

- ## And

    And joins two or more words, phrases, or clauses of similar function and is used to show addition.

    *Like peas **and** broad beans, soya beans grow in pods.*

    *The plant is ready for harvesting when the leaves turn yellow and drop off, **and** the pods and stems dry out.*

    Note: When *and* joins two subjects, the verb is plural.

    *Soya beans and peas **have** pods.*

- ## But

    But joins two or more words, phrases, or clauses and is used to show contrast.

    *In the U.S. soya is not harvested by hand **but** by machine.*

    *Soya is not a new discovery **but** is one of the oldest crops grown in the Orient.*

- ## Or

    Or joins two or more words, phrases, or clauses. It is used to give a choice.

    *The beans may be yellow, green, brown, **or** mottled.*

    *After being chilled, the margarine is packed into tubs **or** cut in blocks.*

- ## So

    So joins a clause. It does not join single words or phrases. *So* is used to show effect.

    *The soya bean is versatile, **so** it is grown widely.*

Strategy

Although other conjunctions are not tested directly in the Structure section, some conjunctive adverbs like *moreover, nevertheless,* and *therefore* may appear in the distractors, in which case they will be the wrong choice. However, when these words appear with conjunctions like *and, but,* or *or,* they may be used to join clauses.

Example: and therefore
  but nevertheless
  and moreover

CORRELATIVE CONJUNCTIONS

Like coordinating conjunctions, these words are used to join words, phrases, and clauses. Correlative conjunctions or paired conjunctions appear in two parts:

> either . . . or
> neither . . . nor
> both . . . and
> not only . . . but also
> whether . . . or

Each of the pair of words should be followed by a word of the same grammatical form.

Either (noun) *or* (noun)
Not only (adj) *but also* (adj)

- *Either . . . or*

  Either . . . or is used to indicate alternatives.

  *Soya can be used in **either** fish feed **or** chicken feed.*

  The subject closest to the verb will determine if the verb is singular or plural.

- *Neither . . . nor*

  Neither . . . nor is used to indicate negative alternatives.

  *Soya is dangerous to **neither** humans **nor** animals.*

  The subject closest to the verb will determine if the verb is singular or plural.

- *Both . . . and*

    Both . . . and indicates addition.

    Soya protein isolate is used in **both** *meat* **and** *fish products.*

    Subjects connected with *both . . . and* take a plural verb.

- *Not only . . . but also*

    Not only . . . but also emphasizes addition.

    Soya is **not only** *the most efficient* **but also** *the least costly source of protein.*

    The *not only* clause must come before the phrase it refers to. The subject closest to the verb will determine if the verb is singular or plural.

- *Whether . . . or*

    Whether . . . or indicates a condition.

    Whether *it is in the print of a newspaper* **or** *the food we eat, our lives are touched by soya.*

EXERCISE 3   Answers on page 192

> ### Choose the one word or phrase that best completes the sentence.

1. Around 1910 chemists and manufacturers came to recognize the value of the soya bean, _____ the great soya processing industry was born.

    (A) with
    (B) and
    (C) but
    (D) or

2. The expansion of the industry was not only due to the world shortage of edible oils, _____ to the Second World War, which put traditional sources of protein in short supply.

    (A) but also
    (B) as well as
    (C) and so
    (D) but also as

3. Research began in the United States into ways of using soya meal for human food, _____ it was not until the 1950s that the first edible soya protein was produced.

   (A) nevertheless
   (B) or
   (C) but
   (D) and

4. The soya plant is an annual, _____ new seeds must be planted every year.

   (A) such
   (B) and since
   (C) while
   (D) so

5. The soya plant is attacked by both fungus disease _____ virus disease.

   (A) and
   (B) and also
   (C) but also
   (D) or

6. The ground bran from soya is used either in breakfast cereals _____ in animal feed.

   (A) nor
   (B) or
   (C) and also
   (D) and

7. Soya protein isolate is used where a high level of protein is required, whether it is dietetic _____ hospital food.

   (A) or
   (B) nor
   (C) and also
   (D) but also

8. Today most margarine is made of vegetable oils _____ originally it was made from animal fats.

   (A) except
   (B) but
   (C) nevertheless
   (D) thus

On the TOEFL® Test

In the Structure section errors with conjunctions include:

1. Coordinating conjunctions:

   and (addition)
   but (contrast)
   or (choice)

2. Correlative conjunctions:

   either . . . or
   neither . . . nor
   both . . . and
   not only . . . but also
   whether . . . or

Since correlative conjunctions are in two parts, there is usually an error in one of the parts.

Example: Soya is an important crop used in _____ food and industrial processes.

(A) either
(B) both
(C) and
(D) just

The best answer is (B). The correct construction is *both . . . and;* the other distractors do not follow this construction.

In the Written Expression section errors with conjunctions also include:

1. Coordinating conjunctions: *and, but, or*

2. Correlative conjunctions: *either . . . or, neither . . . nor, both . . . and, not only . . . but also, whether . . . or*

Example: Soya beans contain not only vitamins and also important
      A   B   C   D
      minerals.

The correct answer is (C). The correct construction is *not only . . . but also.*

EXERCISES ON CONJUNCTIONS   Answers on page 192

> **Choose the one word or phrase that best completes the sentence.**

1. Both diamond _____ graphite are made of the same element, which is carbon.

   (A) and
   (B) except
   (C) together
   (D) both

2. Blinking helps keep the surface of the eye clean _____ moist.

   (A) to
   (B) or
   (C) and
   (D) so

3. Normally, piranhas swim alone and feed on smaller fish _____ on seeds in the water.

   (A) but
   (B) either
   (C) instead
   (D) or

4. Most rodents eat grain, seeds, and nuts, _____ some eat almost anything.

   (A) contrary
   (B) they
   (C) but
   (D) instead

5. Fungi do not absorb sunlight but use animals and plants, _____ dead and living, as their source of food.

   (A) furthermore
   (B) both
   (C) together
   (D) besides

6. Recently doctors warned that too much animal fat in the diet can lead to heart disease, _____ special types of margarine made with vegetable oils are becoming popular.

   (A) because
   (B) so
   (C) and since
   (D) except

Choose the one underlined word or phrase that must be changed for the sentence to be correct.

7. Peppermint originated in Europe, not only the early English colonists
     A   B
   brought it to North America.
    C   D

8. The central core of the earth is made of both very hot or dense material.
        A   B   C   D

9. Many meteorite falls go unnoticed because they either happen at night
    A   B   C
   nor they hit the earth in uninhabited areas.
    D

10. Octopuses have not only large brains and also a well-developed nervous
         A   B   C   D
    system.

11. Most scholars are unsure whether the wheel was first used by potters in
     A   B   C
    Mesopotamia and in the central or eastern parts of Europe.
                 D

12. Compact discs are affected neither by scratching and by dust.
               A   B   C   D

CHAPTER 13

PARALLEL STRUCTURE

Introduction: Vitamin C

In the past people suffered from a disease called scurvy. Their gums bled, their skin became rough, their wounds did not heal, and their muscles wasted away. The cause of these symptoms was a lack of vitamin C; people ate preserved meats and foods and could not get fresh vegetables and fruits.

The best sources of vitamin C are oranges, lemons, grapefruit, cantaloupes, strawberries, and fresh vegetables. These fruits must be fresh because vitamin C is destroyed by heat, storage, or exposure to air.

Although today more people take vitamin C pills than any other supplement, some people still have scurvy, including some of the elderly, alcoholics, and the chronically ill.

Research shows that vitamin C reduces the severity of colds and can help prevent cancer. There is also evidence that vitamin C prevents heart disease, speeds wound healing, helps prevent gum disease, and helps protect us from pollutants such as cigarette smoke. Some recent research also shows that vitamin C has a positive effect on some mental disorders and increases life span.

EXERCISE 1   Answers on page 192

> **Parallel Structure is tested on the TOEFL® test. Complete the following sentences with words from the passage that have parallel structure.**

1. In the past, people got scurvy because they did not get
   _____ and _____.

2. When people got scurvy their _____, _____,
   _____, and _____.

3. Vitamin C is destroyed by _____, _____, or
   _____.

4. Today some people like _____, _____, and
   _____ have scurvy.

---

5. There is evidence that vitamin C prevents heart disease,
_____, _____, and _____.

6. Recent research shows that vitamin C helps some mental disorders and
_____.

EXERCISE 2   Answers on page 192

Correct the claims for and against vitamin C supplements by putting them in parallel form. Use the simple present tense for the verbs.

For

1. Lowering cholesterol and fights heart disease.

2. Helps to keep good eyesight.

3. Protects against smoking and various pollutants.

4. Diabetes fights.

5. Will fight gum disease.

6. Strengthen immunity against colds.

Against

1. Is a waste of money because the body excretes excess vitamin C.

2. Will cause kidney stones or gout in some people.

3. May cause diarrhea and stomach cramps in some people.

4. Causes stones in the bladder in some people.

Grammar: Parallel Structure

Many sentences present information in a series or list. The series may have two, three, or more parts that all have the same grammatical structure. This is known as parallel structure.

Strategy

Make sure that words in a sequence have the same form. These may be nouns, adjectives, verbs, adverbs, phrases, and so on.

• Series Containing Nouns, Adjectives, Verbs, Adverbs, or Phrases

Nouns:	*Vitamin C is destroyed by **heat, storage,** or **exposure** to air.*
Adjectives:	*The criticism that taking vitamin C supplements is a waste of money is considered to be **inaccurate** and **unwarranted** by some.*
Verbs:	*There is evidence that vitamin C **prevents** heart disease, **speeds** wound healing, and **helps** gum disease.*
Adverbs:	*Vitamin supplements can be prepared **naturally** and **synthetically.***
Phrases:	*Large amounts of vitamin C can be bought **in the form of crystals** or **in the form of granules.***

• Gerunds or Infinitives

Gerund:	*Claims for vitamin C such as **reducing** stress and **improving** athletic performance have not been scientifically demonstrated.*
Infinitive:	*When people get scurvy their cells tend **to disintegrate** and **to fall apart.***

• Correlative Conjunctions

both . . . and	neither . . . nor
either . . . or	not only . . . but also

***Both** fruits **and** vegetables are rich sources of vitamin C.*
*Since vitamin A is not created in the body, it must be supplied by **either** food **or** supplements.*

EXERCISE 3   Answers on page 192

> **The following sentences contain a series. Underline the parallel structure, then decide what type of series the sentence contains by using the following abbreviations: nouns (N), verbs (V), adjectives (ADJ), adverbs (ADV).**

1. Vitamin E protects against heart disease, prevents cancer, and fights skin problems.

2. The mineral fluoride is found naturally in soils, water, plants, and animal tissue.

3. The tomato plant needs a long growing season and light, rich, well-drained soil.

4. Vitamin E is being employed slowly but steadily in medicine in an expanding range of ailments.

5. Studies have shown that vitamin C can reduce the severity and length of colds, but not the number of colds a person gets.

6. If you do not have enough iron, you can suffer from anemia, which makes you pale, tired, and weak.

EXERCISE 4   Answers on page 192

Underline the errors in parallel structure in the following sentences.

1. Iron-deficiency anemia has been implicated in emotion, social, and learning difficulties in infants, adolescents, and adults.

2. All "B" vitamins are needed for a healthy appetite, energy production in cells, healthy nervous, and skin.

3. Some vitamins may cause toxic, allergy reactions in some people.

4. Symptoms of a mild case of vitamin C deficiency may be weakness, irritable, loss of weight, and apathy.

5. Claims that vitamin C will prevent, relief, or cure colds and winter illnesses are unwarranted, according to Hodges.

6. Magnesium deficiency is characterized by loss of appetite, nausea, confusing, loss of coordination, and tremors.

EXERCISE 5   Answers on page 193

Identify and correct errors in parallel structure related to *infinitives* and *gerunds* in the following sentences.

1. Some people take vitamin E to relieve muscular cramps, to extend life span, and fighting skin problems.

2. The Nobel laureate Dr. Linus Pauling persistently claimed that vitamin C is effective in preventing and alleviating colds and to treat cancer.

3. Many food processes such as drying, flavoring, canning, and to tenderize may add salt.

4. It is important to select foods that are in their best state, storing them properly, and prepare them to ensure the maximum retention of vitamin C.

5. Avoiding the purchase of foods with salt content while marketing or to eat out is helpful.

6. The major function of vitamin D is to ensure an adequate supply of calcium and phosphorus in the bones, to prevent rickets in children, and maintaining good levels of calcium and phosphorus in the blood.

EXERCISE 6   Answers on page 193

Identify and correct errors in parallel structure related to correlative conjunctions in the following sentences.

1. Very large intakes of any of the essential nutrients may result in both undesirable toxic symptoms and seriously side effects.

2. Minerals in the cell influence not only the vital processes of oxidation but also secreting and growth.

3. Many people feel that both frozen and can fruits and vegetables are inferior to fresh produce.

4. Canned food can be kept neither for unlimited lengths of time nor any temperature.

5. Fruit grown either sheltered from sunlight or growing in a season of many rainy days will not have much vitamin C.

6. Good peaches should be neither too hard, nor too softness.

On the TOEFL® Test

Parallel structure is tested in both the Structure section and the Written Expression section. Words in parallel structure must have the same form in a sequence. In the Structure section, look for words in choices (A), (B), (C), and (D) that follow the same form as in the main sentence.

Example: Vitamin C boosts immunity against colds, _____ asthma, and helps maintain good vision.

(A) counteracting
(B) counteracts
(C) will counteract
(D) it is counteractive to

The best answer is (B). *Counteracts* is parallel with the other items in the sequence: *boosts* immunity and *helps* maintain good vision. Choices (A), (C), and (D) are not in the simple present tense and therefore are not parallel.

In the Written Expression section, sentences have the same errors in parallel structure as in the Structure section. Sentences have a sequence of three or more items, but here one of the items in the sequence is not grammatically parallel with the other items in the sequence.

Example: Symptoms of mild vitamin C deficiency may be <u>weakness</u>,
A

<u>irritability</u>, <u>losing weight</u>, and <u>apathy</u>.
B   C   D

The best answer is (C). Losing weight is not parallel with the other items in the series: *losing* is a gerund whereas the other items are nouns.

EXERCISES ON PARALLEL STRUCTURE   Answers on page 193

> ## Choose the one underlined word or phrase that must be changed for the sentence to be correct.

1. In the <u>human body</u>, phosphorus compounds are found chiefly in
   A

   <u>the bones</u>, <u>brain</u>, and <u>nervous</u>.
   B   C   D

2. Pipelines are continually inspected for leaks and <u>for damage</u> caused by
   A

   such conditions as <u>freezing temperatures</u>, <u>heavy rain</u>, and <u>soil erode</u>.
   B   C   D

3. <u>The sounds</u> produced by a <u>musical instrument</u>, <u>to whistle</u>, or a siren
   A   B   C

   have seven <u>frequencies</u> at the same time.
   D

4. Plastics used to make textiles can <u>be drawn</u> into <u>fine threads</u>, then
   A   B

   <u>woven</u> or <u>knit</u> into fabrics.
   C   D

5. <u>Insufficient protein</u> in the diet may cause a <u>lack of energy</u>,
   A   B

   <u>stunted growth</u>, and <u>lowering resistance to disease</u>.
   C   D

6. <u>Chemical substances</u> called hormones, many of which are proteins,
   A

   control such processes as <u>growth</u>, <u>develop</u>, and <u>reproduction</u>.
   B   C   D

Choose the one word or phrase that best completes the sentence.

7. To qualify as a language, a communication system must have the features of meaningfulness, _____, and productivity.

   (A) displacement
   (B) to displace
   (C) displacing
   (D) to be displaced

8. Many mental disorders are believed to result from a combination of emotional, _____, and biological factors.

   (A) society
   (B) social
   (C) socially
   (D) to be social

9. A neuron cell can not only receive messages from sense organs, but it can also

   _____.

   (A) to transmit messages throughout the body.
   (B) by transmitting messages throughout the body
   (C) transmit messages throughout the body
   (D) a transmitter of messages throughout the body

10. Morse invented a code in which letters, numbers, and _____ are changed into short and long signals called dots and dashes.

    (A) punctuate
    (B) punctuating
    (C) to punctuate
    (D) punctuation

11. Hormones have many jobs, from promoting bodily growth to _____ to regulating metabolism.

    (A) aid digestion
    (B) aiding digestion
    (C) be of aid to digestion
    (D) an aid of digestion

12. Thomas Malthus claimed that disease, war, famine, and _____ act as checks on population growth.

    (A) moral restraining
    (B) morally restrain
    (C) moral restraint
    (D) by moral restraint

CHAPTER

14 *WORD ORDER*

Introduction: Computers

It is relatively easy for computers to speak. A computer that says "please" and "thank you" in the right places is no miracle of science, but recognizing the words that make up normal, continuous human speech is another matter.

Not until now have computers been programmed to react to a range of spoken commands. Until recently it was thought that computers would have to be programmed to the accent and speech habits of each user, and only then would be able to respond accurately to their master's or mistress's voice. Now rapid progress is being made with systems programmed to adapt easily to each new speaker.

The IBM Tangora system, under development at the end of the 1980s, was claimed to recognize a spoken vocabulary of 20,000 words with 95 percent accuracy. The system included a processor that could make informed guesses as to what is a likely sentence. The system had been programmed not only with grammatical rules, but also with an analysis of a vast quantity of office correspondence. On the basis of this information, the machine could calculate the probability of one particular word following another.

Statistical probability is necessary for computers to interpret not only speech but also visual data. Security systems can distinguish between faces they have been taught to recognize, but never has a computer been able to match a human's ability to make sense of a three-dimensional scene by identifying all objects in it.

EXERCISE 1   Answers on page 193

Word order is tested on the TOEFL® test. Correct the word order in the following sentences.

1. For computers to speak relatively easy is.

2. Until recently it thought was computers would have to be programmed to the accent and speech habits of the user.

3. It is claimed that the IBM Tangora system can recognize a vocabulary spoken of 20,000 words.

4. Statistical probability necessary is for computers to interpret not only speech but visual data as well.

5. Up to now have computers not been programmed to react to a range of spoken commands.

6. The machine can calculate the probability of one word particular following another.

EXERCISE 2   Answers on page 193

With sentences starting with a negative word, word order is reversed. Complete the sentences with the correct negative word.

1. (Not until/Never) now have computers been programmed to react to spoken commands.

2. (Never/Not only) has a computer been able to match a human's ability to make sense of a three-dimensional scene.

3. (Only/Not only) are grammatical rules programmed into the computer but also an analysis of office correspondence.

4. (Not until/Scarcely) recently was it thought that computers would have to be programmed to the speech and accent of the user.

5. (Only/No sooner than) recently has progress been made in recognizing human speech.

Grammar: Word Order

INVERSION

In English the usual word order is

subject (S) + verb (V) + object (O)

In some situations the order is changed, and the verb is placed before the subject.

- In a question the subject follows the aux-word or verb.

Usual word order: *You are using* a *computer*.
$$\underset{S}{} \quad \underset{V}{} \quad \underset{O}{}$$

Inversion: *Are you using a computer?*
$$\underset{S}{} \qquad \underset{O}{}$$

- When there is a prepositional phrase indicating place at the beginning of a sentence, inversion occurs.

Usual word order:	*The workings of the computer are **inside** the system unit.*
Inversion:	***Inside** the system unit are the workings of the computer.*
Usual word order:	*The computer programs are fed **into** the computer.*
Inversion:	***Into** the computer are fed the computer programs.*

- When the conditional "if" has been omitted, inverted word order is correct.

Usual word order:	*If I had used a computer it would have been finished now.*
Inversion:	*Had I used a computer, it would have been finished now.*
Usual word order:	*If you should need the information, it will be in the computer.*
Inversion:	*Should you need the information, it will be in the computer.*

• When a statement begins with a negative word or phrase, inversion occurs.

When the words below begin a sentence or an independent clause, there is a change in word order.

never	only
nor	only after
neither	only once
hardly ever	only once
no sooner than	only in this way
not often only	only then
not only . . . as well	rarely
not only . . . but also	scarcely
not until	seldom
nowhere	under no circumstances
on no account	so

Usual word order: *I will **never** again write on a typewriter.*

Inversion: ***Never** again will I write on a typewriter.*

Usual word order: *The computer **not only** examines information **but also** performs logical operations.*

Inversion: ***Not only** does the computer examine information **but** it **also** performs logical operations.*

EXERCISE 3   Answers on page 193

Rewrite the sentences with inverted word order.

1. If you should make an error, it can be corrected easily.

2. Information is stored on a magnetic disk.

3. If he had been more careful, we would not have lost all that data.

4. The computer not only stores information but also distributes it.

5. Personal computers no sooner were invented than typewriters began to be replaced.

6. The impact of the computer has been strongly felt only recently.

OTHER WORDS REVERSED ON THE TOEFL® TEST

> ### Strategy
>
> Be aware that other words such as nouns, adverbs, and adjectives are reversed in order in the Written Expression section.

Other words that are reversed in order that appear in the Written Expression section may include:

- Noun/adjective

Correct:	*important information*
Error:	*information important*

- Adjective/adverb

Correct:	*an extremely accurate document*
Error:	*an accurate extremely document*

- Relative pronoun/preposition

Correct:	*It has transformed the way in which people work.*
Error:	*It has transformed the way which in people work.*

- Enough plus adjective

Correct:	*simple enough*
Error:	*enough simple*

- Indirect questions

Correct:	*He asked how expensive it was.*
Error:	*He asked how expensive was it.*

- Participle/adverb

Correct:	*an accurately typed document*
Error:	*a typed accurately document*

- Adjective/adverb

Correct:	*increasingly important machine*
Error:	*important increasingly machine*

EXERCISE 4   Answers on page 193

> **Choose the one underlined word or phrase that must be changed for the sentence to be correct.**

1. The development of <u>voice</u> recognition <u>will</u> enable the computer
                   A   B
   <u>to respond</u> to <u>commands spoken</u>.
       C   D

2. The keyboard with <u>alphabet</u> keys is <u>enough easy</u> <u>to use</u> to give <u>program</u>
                       A   B   C   D
   instructions to the computer.

3. Computers <u>are</u> <u>machines flexible</u> that <u>can adapt</u> to a <u>wide</u> variety of tasks.
             A   B   C   D

4. Computers <u>can</u> <u>also</u> produce <u>complex</u> and <u>original highly</u> music.
            A B   C   D

5. Images and sounds <u>often</u> <u>added are</u> to games <u>to make</u> them
                     A   B   C
   <u>more realistic</u> and more exciting.
      D

On the TOEFL® Test

> In the Written Expression section, word order problems involve two words in reverse order. These words may be:

1. Adjective/noun

2. Main verb/auxiliary

3. Enough/adjective

4. Indirect question word order

5. Adjective/adverb

6. Participle/adverb

7. Relative pronoun/preposition

   Example: A <u>pocket</u> computer is <u>generally</u> <u>enough</u> small to fit into a
             A   B   C
           pocket or a <u>small</u> case.
                    D

The best answer is (C). The correct word order is adjective + enough: *small enough.*

In the Structure section, word order problems involve sentences beginning with negative words or conditionals.

Example: _____ used for making decisions in the business world, but also for forecasting and planning.

(A) Not only are computers
(B) Computers are
(C) Not only computers are
(D) Only computers are

The best answer is (A). Reversed subject/verb order is needed in sentences beginning with the negative *not only . . . but also* construction.

EXERCISES ON WORD ORDER   Answers on page 194

> **Choose the one underlined word or phrase that must be changed for the sentence to be correct.**

1. In the nineteenth century, Ada Lovelace <u>devised</u> several <u>computer</u>
                                        A   B
   programs for a calculating machine <u>which in</u> coded cards <u>were used</u>.
                                        C   D

2. In 1821, Babbage found <u>it</u> difficult <u>to make</u> a machine's parts
                              A   B
   <u>enough accurate</u> <u>to prevent</u> errors in calculation.
      C   D

3. <u>Does seldom</u> a <u>computer</u> <u>make</u> a <u>mistake</u>.
      A   B   C   D

4. Science <u>is</u> the process of <u>gathering</u> knowledge and answering <u>questions</u>
         A   B   C
   about the world and how <u>works it</u>.
                       D

5. The telescope <u>first</u> used <u>was</u> in 1608 <u>as</u> a war weapon <u>to spy</u> on enemy
                   A   B   C   D
   ships.

6. <u>When</u> the weather <u>is</u> warm, or during <u>exercise strenuous</u>, the sweat
     A   B   C
   glands <u>increase</u> their production.
          D

Choose the one word or phrase that best completes the sentence.

7. _____ reptiles hunt at temperatures of 12°C or below.

(A) Seldom do
(B) Do seldom
(C) Do
(D) Seldom

8. _____ learn during their sleep by listening to tape recordings.

(A) People rarely can
(B) Can people rarely
(C) Rarely can people
(D) Can rarely people

9. _____ continental crust older than 200 million years.

(A) It is nowhere the
(B) Nowhere is the
(C) Is nowhere the
(D) Is the nowhere

10. _____ lay its eggs in the sand on the beach than it goes back to the sea.

(A) No sooner a turtle does
(B) A turtle does no sooner
(C) Does no sooner a turtle
(D) No sooner does a turtle

11. _____ in medicine relieve distress but they also prevent and cure illness.

(A) Not only do computers
(B) Do computers
(C) Computers
(D) Computers not only

12. Not only _____ in the field of psychology but animal behavior is examined as well.

(A) human behavior is studied
(B) is human behavior studied
(C) is studied human behavior
(D) human behavior

WORD FORMS

Introduction: Benjamin Franklin

Benjamin Franklin was an American politician, inventor, and scientist. He was born in 1706 and at the age of ten set to work in his father's candle and soap business. However, he disliked his work and two years later he went to work for a printer. He eventually became a successful printer, producing a weekly newspaper and popular books. He also became a politician and helped the United States become free from British rule. His inventions included a smokeless stove, bifocal lenses, and new types of fertilizer.

In 1752 Franklin conducted a dangerous experiment. By flying a kite during a storm, he discovered that a lightning bolt is just a large electric spark. Franklin put his discovery to use and invented the lightning conductor. This is a thick metal wire that ran from the top of a building to the ground. If lightning struck the building, the electricity would travel down the wire to the ground and therefore would not damage the building or harm the people inside. This discovery was the first step in developing ways of making use of electricity to power machines.

EXERCISE 1   Answers on page 194

> **Word forms are tested on the TOEFL® test. Fill in the blanks with the correct words from the reading.**

1. Franklin was a famous politician and _____.

2. After working in his father's business, he worked for a _____.

3. Later he became a _____ and helped the United States become free from the British.

4. In 1752 Franklin did a _____ experiment by flying a kite in a storm.

5. A lightning conductor was a _____ _____ wire that ran from the top of a building to the ground.

6. What Franklin discovered during the storm was put to good _____ by his invention of the lightning conductor.

EXERCISE 2   Answers on page 194

From the reading on page 133 decide whether these statements are *true* or *false*.

1. Benjamin Franklin was not a success as a printer.   T F

2. Benjamin Franklin is famous only in politics and for his invention of fertilizers.   T F

3. Franklin's kite experiment in a storm was dangerous.   T F

4. The lightning conductor is a thick electric wire that runs from the top of a building to the ground.   T F

5. Franklin discovered that lightning is electricity.   T F

6. Franklin's discovery helped to develop ways of using electricity as a source of power.   T F

Grammar: Word Forms

It is important to know if a word is a noun, a verb, an adjective, or an adverb. This is one of the most common types of error tested in the Written Expression section. As many as 20 percent of the items in this part of the test may be word form problems. These errors involve using one part of speech for another—a noun instead of a verb, an adjective instead of an adverb, and so on.

The form of a word depends on its position in a sentence. Look at how the word *electricity* changes form.

Noun form: ***Electricity** traveled down the wire.*
Verb form: *Franklin was not **electrocuted** by lightning.*
Adjective form: *An **electrical** current ran down the wire.*
Adverb form: *The machine runs **electrically**.*

NOUNS

Nouns can be identified by their position and/or function in a sentence. Knowing noun endings (suffixes) will also help identify nouns.

Strategy

Remember the correct noun form for a field of study and the name of the person who practices in that field.

NOUN ENDINGS FOR PEOPLE:
Connected with a place or thing:

| *-ian* | politician |
| *-ist* | scientist |

People who do things:

-ee	employee
-er	printer
-or	inventor

NOUNS CONNECTED WITH FIELDS OF STUDY:

-ogy	biology
-ic(s)	politics
-ation	administration
-y	chemistry
-ce	science

EXERCISE 3   Answers on page 194

Choose the correct word in parentheses.

1. Franklin was a (politics/politician).

2. Franklin was also an (invention/inventor).

3. Franklin is known in the field of (science/scientist).

4. Franklin became a successful (printer/printing).

5. In 1820 a Danish (physicist/physics) proved that electricity produced magnetism.

6. One scientist who helped modern (chemist/chemistry) was Antoine Lavoisier.

   Other noun endings (suffixes) include:

-acy	-en	-in	-ling
-age	-ess	-ing	-ment
-ance/ence	-ful	-ion	-ness
-ant/ent	-hood	-ism	-ocracy
-ate	-ia	-ite	-ry(ary/ery)
-ation	-ide	-ty	-ship
-dom			-ster
			-ive
			-y/ie

> **Strategy**
>
> Remember the correct noun or verb ending. Avoid confusion between nouns and verbs.

VERBS

Verbs are used to show the action of the subject.

> *Franklin **discovered** that lightning is electricity.*
>
> Verb endings include:

-ate	circulate	*-er*	discover
-en	sharpen	*-ify*	electrify
-ing	developing	*-ize*	politicize
-ed	invented		

EXERCISE 4   Answers on page 194

> **Make verbs from the following words:**

1. active
2. thick
3. sympathy
4. regular
5. solid
6. light

EXERCISE 5   Answers on page 194

> **Look at the underlined verbs or nouns. If the word is not correct, write the correct form.**

1. In Franklin's time, electricity was mainly used as a form of <u>entertain</u>.
2. Franklin wanted <u>free</u> from British rule for the United States.
3. Franklin <u>discovery</u> that lightning was electricity.
4. Franklin was the only man to <u>signature</u> all four key documents that helped to make the United States independent.

5. Besides his many activities in the <u>serve</u> of his country, he found time to be an inventor.

6. Franklin <u>development</u> the first pair of bifocal spectacles.

ADJECTIVES

Adjectives modify or describe nouns. They usually come before nouns or after the verb *to be*. Adjectives usually answer the question "What kind?"

Adjectives have only *one* form, which is used with both singular and plural nouns.

*Franklin was a **brave** scientist.*

Adjective endings include:

-al/ial	-ing
-able/ible	-ish
-ant/ent	-ive
-ary	-less
-ory	-like
-ed	-ly
-er	-some
-ful	-ous
-ic	-worthy
-ile	-y

Strategy

The most common type of word form error occurs when an adjective is used as an adverb or an adverb is used as an adjective. Keep in mind that an adjective answers the question "What kind?" and an adverb answers the question "How?" Look at the endings of adjectives and adverbs.

ADVERBS

Adverbs modify verbs, adverbs, and adjectives. Adverbs usually answer the question "How?" Adverbs are often formed by adding *-ly* to an adjective.

Adjective: *brave*
Adverb: *bravely*

Exceptions: The adverbs *hard, fast,* and *high* have the same form as adjectives.

Some adjectives end in *-ly* like adverbs: *friendly, costly, yearly.*

Adverb endings include:
-ly
-ward
-wise

EXERCISE 6   Answers on page 194

> **Choose the correct adjective or adverb in parentheses.**

1. Franklin became a (successfully/successful) printer.

2. At age 40, Franklin became (interested/interestingly) in electricity.

3. Franklin produced a (week/weekly) newspaper and many popular books.

4. The lightning conductor attracted lightning and carried it (safe/safely) to the ground.

5. Among his many inventions was a (smokelessly/smokeless) stove.

6. Franklin put his invention to (well/good) use.

EXERCISE 7   Answers on page 194

> **Identify the following words as a *noun (N)*, a *verb (V)*, an *adjective (ADJ)*, or an *adverb (ADV)*.**

1. dangerous _____

2. electricity _____

3. invention _____

4. scientist _____

5. successful _____

6. experiment _____

7. discovery _____

8. development _____

9. brilliantly _____

10. conductor _____

Exercise 8   Answers on page 194

Identify the underlined word as a *noun* (N), a *verb* (V), an *adjective* (ADJ), or an *adverb* (ADV).

1. Benjamin Franklin was <u>cautious</u> in performing his famous kite experiment.

2. The first two men who tried to repeat Franklin's experiment were <u>electrocuted</u>.

3. He flew a kite fitted with a <u>metal</u> key into a storm cloud.

4. Franklin <u>eventually</u> became a successful printer.

5. When <u>lightning</u> hit the key, sparks flew off it.

6. Franklin proved that storm clouds are <u>charged</u> with electricity.

7. Lightning is caused by the <u>discharge</u> of electricity in the form of a spark.

8. Franklin was able to prove that storm clouds have <u>static</u> electricity.

On the TOEFL® Test

In the Written Expression section, the most common errors tested are word form errors. Of these, the most frequent are listed below:

1. The use of an adjective instead of an adverb or an adverb instead of an adjective.

   Example: Around 1750, <u>electricity</u> <u>experiments</u> became <u>popularly</u> as
                            A   B   C
   <u>entertainment</u> at the court of the French King, Louis XV.
       D

   The best answer is (C). An adjective, *popular,* not an adverb, is required.

   Example: In 1780, Italian <u>scientist</u> Luigi Galvani <u>mistaken</u> concluded
                              A   B
   that frogs' legs <u>contain</u> <u>electricity</u>.
                     C   D

   The correct answer is (B). An adverb, *mistakenly,* is needed to modify the verb *concluded.*

2. The name of a field of study is mistakenly used for the person who practices it, or a field of study is confused with an adjective describing it.

Example: As well as being <u>successful</u> in his many <u>careers</u>, Benjamin
                              A   B
              Franklin was <u>well-known</u> as a <u>science</u>.
                          C   D

The best answer is (D). *Science* is the name of the field. The correct answer is *scientist,* the name of the person who practices in the field.

3. Other word form errors include the use of incorrect forms for nouns, verbs, adjectives, and adverbs.

Example: Electricity produced by <u>nature</u> is called <u>static</u> electricity
                               A   B
           because it exerts a <u>forceful</u> when it is <u>stationary</u>.
                         C   D

The best answer is (C). The noun *force,* not the adjective *forceful,* is needed.

Example: When lightning strikes an <u>unprotected</u> building, the <u>electric</u>
                                  A   B
          charge can cause <u>considering</u> <u>damage</u>.
                      C   D

The correct answer is (C). The adjective *considerable* is needed instead of the gerund *considering.*

EXERCISES ON WORD FORMS   Answers on page 194

> **Choose the one underlined word or phrase that must be changed for the sentence to be correct.**

1. <u>Diamonds</u> are graded according to <u>weigh</u>, <u>color</u>, and <u>cut</u>.
   A   B   C   D

2. As an <u>educator</u>, John Dewey opposed the <u>traditional</u> method of learning
         A   B
   by <u>memory</u> under the <u>authorize</u> of teachers.
        C   D

3. A <u>substantial</u> <u>proportional</u> of the <u>printers</u> and newspaper publishers in
     A   B   C
   <u>colonial</u> America were women.
     D

4. Many seeds remain <u>dormantly</u> in the ground until conditions <u>involving</u>
                     A   B

    <u>heat</u> and water are correct for <u>germination</u>.
     C   D

5. Lavoisier was the first to recognize the <u>importance</u> of <u>accurately</u>
                                            A   B

    measurements when studying <u>chemical</u> <u>changes</u>.
                                   C   D

6. Nails act as a <u>hard</u> base for the <u>sensitive</u> skin of the fingertips and toe
                    A   B

    tips to press against, so they may help our <u>sensitively</u> to <u>touch</u>.
                                                 C   D

7. Lichens can survive <u>extremes</u> of <u>heat</u>, <u>cold</u>, and <u>dry</u>.
                              A   B   C   D

8. Diamond is the <u>hardest</u> known mineral, <u>whereas</u> graphite is very <u>soft</u>
                   A   B   C

    and <u>flake</u>.
        D

9. <u>Medicine</u> in the future will make increasing use of high <u>technology</u> for
     A   B

    the <u>investigate</u> and diagnosis of illnesses, as well as for their <u>treatment</u>.
        C   D

10. Herman Melville's work, which is <u>complexity</u>, <u>philosophical</u>, and
                                         A   B

    <u>humorous</u>, is recognized as one of the most astonishing <u>achievements</u> in
     C   D

    all American literature.

11. Cells carry out the <u>essentially</u> <u>processes</u> that produce <u>energy</u> and <u>sustain</u>
                          A   B   C   D

    life.

12. Like their ancestors, most sharks are <u>streamline</u>, <u>fast-swimming</u> <u>hunters</u>
                                        A   B   C

    living in the upper waters of <u>warm</u> seas.
                                  D

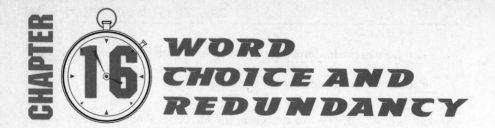
Introduction: Asbestos

Asbestos is a type of mineral found in rocks that has a fibrous structure and so can be woven. Unlike other flexible woven material, it is capable of withstanding very high temperatures while at the same time deflecting heat. Woven metal wire, for example, might do the first job, but would not do the second. For this reason, asbestos gloves, suits, and shields have been vital for protection in fire fighting. There are hundreds of uses for asbestos in industry and construction. Asbestos can be mixed with other materials, such as rubber, graphite, paint, and cement, for special purposes that demand extra flexibility, slipperiness, coating quality, or hardness. Asbestos is so useful that it was once found in almost all modern buildings and machines. Modern industry has also benefited from its uses as a material for electrical and sound insulation.

The unique properties of asbestos have led to its continued but restricted use. In this century, industries in the United States alone have used more than 30 million tons of asbestos. However, after 1950, health warnings about asbestos began to appear. Its small fibers, so useful in other respects, could also be inhaled and lodge in the lungs to cause a disease called asbestosis. This disease restricts normal breathing. Chronic shortness of breath turns sufferers into invalids. Worse still, there is also the risk that lung cancer may follow.

EXERCISE 1 Answers on page 194

Word choice errors are tested on the TOEFL® test. Complete the sentences by choosing the correct words from the reading.

1. Unlike/like other woven material, asbestos is capable of withstanding high temperature while at the same time deflecting heat.

2. Asbestos is such/so useful that it was once used in a lot of modern buildings.

3. After/afterwards 1950, health warnings about asbestos began to appear.

4. Previously asbestos was used in almost/most all modern buildings and machines.

5. Woven metal wire can withstand heat and/but cannot deflect heat.

6. There are hundreds of uses of asbestos in industry and/or construction.

EXERCISE 2 Answers on page 194

A word can have the same meaning as another word, but two words with the same meaning cannot be used together. Match the words in the box with the words underlined in the sentences below.

> A. such as   B. chiefly   C. carefully
> D. beneficial   E. single

1. Asbestos is mainly used in industry and construction.

2. Asbestos can be mixed with other materials, for example, rubber.

3. The small fibers of asbestos, so useful in other ways, could harm the body.

4. Asbestos has some unique qualities.

5. When removing asbestos today, it is important to handle it cautiously.

Grammar: Word Choice

A number of words in English often cause problems because they have similar meanings (make/do) or sound alike (alike/unlike). Many times one word is used incorrectly in place of another.

Strategy

Learn the expressions with *make* and *do*. Whenever you hear a new expression, add it to the list. In the Written Expression section of the test, whenever *make* or *do* is underlined, look for an error.

Make or Do

The verb *to make* means to produce or create, whereas *to do* means to perform, to act. These two verbs are found in a number of expressions.

Expressions with *make* include:

make a mistake	make a plan
make a difference	make an investment
make a comparison	make an offer
make a discovery	make a choice
make use of	make an attempt
make a profit	make a decision
make a suggestion	make a prediction

Expressions with *do* include:

do one's duty	do harm
do homework	do research
do justice to	do an assignment
do business	do one's best
do wrong	do a service
do work	do damage
do a kindness	do wonders

EXERCISE 3   Answers on page 195

Underline the word that correctly completes the sentence.

1. A wide range of new products is now available to (do/make) many of the jobs once (done/made) by materials (made/done) with asbestos.

2. Modern products (made/done) with asbestos look different from the ones that caused problems in the past.

3. Usually radon disperses in the open air and would (do/make) no harm to your body.

4. When radium was mixed with other substances it (made/did) them luminous.

5. Marie Curie (made/did) a great contribution to science through her discovery of radium, although it proved fatal to her.

6. A distinction has been (made/done) between the dangers of blue and white asbestos.

LIKE/ALIKE/UNLIKE

Strategy

Look for the different parts of speech of the words *like/alike/unlike* as well as their different meanings to avoid confusion.

Like is a preposition that means "similar." It is followed by an object.

> *Like many other people, I did not know the dangers of asbestos.*

Alike is an adverb that means "equally"; as an adjective, it means "similar."

> *The new information on asbestos caused panic in construction and industry alike.*

Unlike is a preposition that means "not similar." It is followed by an object.

> *Unlike other woven material, asbestos is capable of withstanding high temperatures and at the same time deflecting heat.*

EXERCISE 4   Answers on page 195

Underline the word that correctly completes the sentence.

1. (Unlike/Alike) blue asbestos, white asbestos is safe when its fibers are sealed off and left undisturbed.

2. Both blue and brown asbestos are (alike/like) in that they are both dangerous.

3. (Like/Alike) all metals, alkaline-earth metals conduct heat and electricity well.

4. Radon, (like/alike) radium, is radioactive.

5. Today synthetic plastic foam is used for insulation, but (unlike/alike) asbestos it cannot be used where there are high temperatures.

6. Asbestos and radium are (alike/like) in that they are both dangerous.

OTHER/THE OTHER/ANOTHER

Another means "one more." It can be used before a singular noun.

> *We need to find **another** way.*

Other means "more of the ones in the group we are talking about." It is used before a plural noun.

> *Asbestos protects **other** materials from fire.*

The other means "the last one of the group we are talking about." It is used before a singular noun, or a noncount noun. It is preceded by a determiner such as *the, some, any, no,* or *one.*

> *No **other** material is capable of withstanding such temperature.*

> *One type of asbestos is dangerous; **the other** type is not as dangerous.*

EXERCISE 5   Answers on page 195

Circle the word that correctly completes the sentence.

1. Another/Other airy material is glass fiber.

2. Ancient Egyptians used asbestos to weave funeral garments for kings and other/another important people.

3. White asbestos, or chyrsolite, is another/other kind of asbestos.

4. Asbestos can be mixed with another/other materials such as rubber, paint, and cement.

5. Other/Another products are now available to do jobs where asbestos was once used.

6. Besides being a good heat and electrical insulator, other/the other use of asbestos has been to keep down noise levels in public buildings.

SO/SUCH/TOO

Both *so . . . that* and *such . . . that* have the same meaning, but they are used with different constructions. *So . . . that* is used with *many, few, much,* and *little.*

> *so* + adverb/adjective + *that*
>
> Asbestos was **so convenient that** everybody used it.
>
> *such* + adjective + noun + *that*
>
> Asbestos had **such unique qualities that** it was used widely.

Too means more than necessary. It comes before an adjective or adverb and is followed by an infinitive.

> Asbestos is **too dangerous** to be used widely.

EXERCISE 6   Answers on page 195

> ### Circle the word that correctly completes the sentence.

1. Asbestos has such/so many properties that it was used in all modern buildings.

2. Asbestos is so/such dangerous that it has been banned in many countries.

3. Asbestos is considered to be so/too dangerous to be used in buildings today.

4. Asbestos was so/too widely used in construction that it is creating problems today.

5. Asbestos can stand such/too high temperatures that it was used as protective clothing by fire fighters.

6. Asbestos is too/so dangerous to be removed without wearing protective clothing or gloves.

MUCH/MANY/FEW/LITTLE

Many and *few* are used with count nouns.

> **Example:** *Many old buildings have asbestos.*

Much and *little* are used with noncount nouns.

> **Example:** *There is **much** caution when dealing with the material today.*

EXERCISE 7   Answers on page 195

Circle the word that correctly completes the sentence.

1. Much/Many blue asbestos is mined in South Africa, Bolivia, and Australia.

2. A small amount of radiation can help cure someone, whereas too much/many will cause harm.

3. Madame Curie, after many/much years of exposure to radium, died of anemia.

4. A little/few radon can be found in much/many types of soil.

5. Few/Little people have had the bad luck to live in an area with a high natural background level of radiation.

6. There was little/few information about the dangers of asbestos before the 1950s.

OTHER COMMONLY CONFUSED WORDS

Strategy

Other words may also be used in word choice errors. The most common words used on the test are listed below. Learn the difference between the words in pairs by looking them up in the dictionary to find out what parts of speech they are and the difference in meaning.

The following words may also be used in word choice problems.

number/amount	near/nearly
few/a few	after/afterward
little/a little	no/not
because/because of	and/but/or
despite/in spite of/although	most/almost
percent/percentage	ago/before
hard/hardly	age/old
twice/double	either . . . or/neither . . . nor
some/somewhat	person/people

EXERCISE 8   Answers on page 195

Circle the word that correctly completes the sentence.

1. An amount/A number of contaminated buildings are known to release dangerous amounts of radioactivity over a period of years.

2. Because of/Although its danger to health, asbestos has been banned in many countries.

3. Synthetic plastic foam should no/not be used where there are high temperatures or any risk of fire.

4. Afterward/After the danger of asbestos was known, glass fiber began to be used widely for heat insulation.

5. Radon is radioactive, and it decays to produce some/somewhat very unhealthy properties.

6. Radon gas is not a threat to human life almost/most of the time.

Grammar: Redundancy

Redundancy is the unnecessary repetition of an idea.

> Correct: *The party proceeded toward the west.*

> Redundant: *The party proceeded forward toward the west.*

The word *proceeded* has the same meaning as *forward*. Therefore, the word *forward* is unnecessary.

The following pairs of words have the same meaning; only one in the pair is necessary.

connect	together	incorrect	mistake
repeat	again	important	significant
join	together	carefully	cautiously
proceed	forward	established	founded
progress	forward	protect	guard
advance	forward	original	first
only	unique	rarely	seldom
new	innovations	transmit	send out
reread	again	single	only
return	back	around	approximately
same	identical	chief	main
sufficient	enough	such as	for example
separated	apart from	necessary	needed

EXERCISE 9   Answers on page 195

> **Circle the number of each sentence that contains a redundant expression.**

1. Asbestos can be mixed with other materials, for example such as rubber, paint, and cement.

2. Because asbestos does not burn and only melts at high temperatures, it can protect and guard other material against fire.

3. One of the main and chief uses of asbestos is to weave gloves, aprons, and other clothing for workers in hot places such as metal foundries.

4. When asbestos fibers are breathed in or swallowed, they can cause serious disease, even cancer.

5. Asbestos shields off, or insulates against, heat, flames, electricity, and noise.

6. The unique and single properties of asbestos mean that it has many important uses.

7. No new innovations have been developed to replace asbestos being used for brake linings on cars.

8. For around approximately thirty years, only white asbestos has been used for protective clothing because it is safer than other forms of asbestos.

On the TOEFL® Test

> Word choice errors that involve the incorrect use of one word for another appear in the Written Expression section. The words given in this chapter are frequently used in word choice errors. Following are some of the most common errors.

1. Wrong use of *so . . . that, such . . . that,* and *too:*

   Example: Asbestos is <u>so</u> a useful material that it was used <u>in</u> <u>almost</u> all

                 A   B   C   D

            modern buildings.

   The best answer is (B). The correct construction is *such* + adjective + noun + *that* clause.

2. Wrong use of *another, other, the other:*

   Example: Other, more common, name for crocidolite is blue asbestos
              ‾‾‾‾‾   ‾‾‾‾‾‾‾‾‾‾‾
                A   B
   because of its color.
   ‾‾‾‾‾‾‾‾ ‾‾‾
      C   D

   The best answer is (A). *Other* is used incorrectly instead of *another.*

3. Wrong use of *make* and *do*

   Example: When asbestos fibers are breathed in, they may make damage
              ‾‾‾‾   ‾‾‾‾‾‾‾   ‾‾‾‾
                A   B   C
   to our lungs.
   ‾‾
      D

   The best answer is (C). The expression is *do damage,* not *make damage.*

EXERCISES ON WORD CHOICE AND REDUNDANCY

Answers on page 195

> **Choose the one underlined word or phrase that must be changed for the sentence to be correct.**

1. About 200 million years before, all the continents were part of one vast
   ‾‾‾‾‾   ‾‾‾‾‾‾‾   ‾‾‾‾‾‾   ‾‾‾‾
     A   B   C   D
   land mass called Pangaea.

2. Investment banks do not accept deposits from the public or do loans to
   ‾‾‾‾‾‾‾‾‾‾   ‾‾‾‾‾‾‾‾   ‾‾‾‾‾‾‾
       A   B   C
   businesses or individuals.
   ‾‾‾‾‾‾‾‾‾‾
       D

3. White blood cells live only for a little days because they are poisoned by
                           ‾‾‾‾   ‾‾‾‾‾‾ ‾‾‾‾‾‾‾
                             A   B   C
   the bacteria they capture.
                     ‾‾‾‾‾‾‾
                        D

4. When actively hunting, a dolphin sends out transmitting about five
   ‾‾‾‾ ‾‾‾‾‾‾‾‾   ‾‾‾‾‾‾‾‾‾‾‾‾
     A   B   C
   signals every second.
           ‾‾‾‾‾
             D

5. A mainframe computer is large and is usually used to operate a network
                                 ‾‾‾   ‾‾‾‾‾‾‾   ‾‾‾‾‾‾‾‾‾‾‾
                                  A   B   C
   of another computers.
      ‾‾‾‾‾‾‾
         D

6. So far <u>most</u> a million <u>different</u> species of insects have been <u>identified</u>
   A   B   C   D
   and named.

7. The sun <u>contains</u> 99.9 <u>percentage</u> of the <u>mass</u> <u>of</u> the solar system.
           A   B   C D

8. Lewis and Clark had <u>been gone</u> for <u>such</u> long on their expedition that
                   A   B
   <u>many</u> thought <u>they</u> were dead.
    C   D

9. A <u>living</u> polyp <u>looks like</u> <u>little</u> sea anemone, with tentacles to trap tiny
    A   B   C
   animals <u>for food</u>.
        D

10. The giant panda eats chiefly <u>mainly</u> bamboo shoots, <u>though</u> it also eats
                         A   B
   some <u>other</u> plants <u>and</u> occasionally feeds on fish and small rodents.
       C   D

11. <u>Most</u> of the Egyptian woman Hypatia's writings on medicine have been
   A
   lost, <u>but</u> there are <u>an amount</u> of references to them by <u>other</u> scientists.
       B   C   D

12. <u>Alike</u> <u>most</u> frogs, the clawed <u>frog</u> catches its prey with <u>its hands</u>.
    A   B   C   D

Part 11

STRUCTURE AND WRITTEN EXPRESSION PRACTICE TESTS

PRACTICE TEST 1

Answers on page 195

Directions

Items in the first part of this section are incomplete sentences. Under each of these sentences, there are four words or phrases. Choose the one word or phrase that best completes the sentence.

EXAMPLE I

Reflexes _____ very valuable in protecting the body against harm.

   (A)   that are
   (B)   being
   (C)   are
   (D)   are being

The best answer is (C). The sentence should read, "Reflexes are very valuable in protecting the body against harm."

EXAMPLE II

Seismographs are used to locate oil, to determine ocean depth, and _____ and measure earthquakes.

   (A)   detect
   (B)   to detect
   (C)   be detecting
   (D)   are detecting

The best answer is (B). The sentence should read, "Seismographs are used to locate oil, to determine ocean depth, and to detect and measure earthquakes."

1. Snakes have an organ in a pit on their heads _____ infrared rays.

   (A) detects
   (B) a detection of
   (C) it detects
   (D) that detects

2. Helium is not flammable _____ therefore safer than hydrogen.

   (A) that is
   (B) and is
   (C) but is
   (D) and it

3. In 1849 Walter Hunt, _____ American inventor, patented a design that served as the basis for modern safety pins.

   (A) an
   (B) he was an
   (C) being
   (D) who was, as an

4. Ansel Adams was a landscape photographer _____ photographs of the western United States show nature on a grand scale.

   (A) whose
   (B) of his
   (C) of whom
   (D) his

5. Contact lenses _____ of acrylic are more transparent and less fragile than lenses made of glass.

   (A) making
   (B) made
   (C) are made
   (D) which make

6. _____ other cells in the body, nerve cells are not healed or replaced when they are damaged or destroyed.

   (A) Different
   (B) Unlikely
   (C) Unlike
   (D) But

7. The higher the content of carbon dioxide in the air, _____.

   (A) more heat it retains
   (B) than it retains more heat
   (C) it retains more heat
   (D) the more heat it retains

8. _____ most brilliant Greek inventor was Archimedes, who lived about 2,250 years ago.

   (A) The
   (B) One of the
   (C) As the
   (D) Of the

9. _____ flying, a bat emits a rapid series of ultrasonic signals, which bounce off any object in its path.

   (A) When it
   (B) When it is
   (C) It is
   (D) When is

10. _____ does not circle around the earth was proven by Galileo.

    (A) Since the rest of the universe
    (B) As the rest of the universe
    (C) The rest of the universe
    (D) That the rest of the universe

11. _____ cell in the body is far from a capillary.

   (A) Not
   (B) No
   (C) Not only a
   (D) Neither a

12. Ralph Waldo Emerson's belief _____ the individual freedom of all people greatly influenced later American thinkers.

   (A) as of
   (B) on
   (C) in
   (D) as in

13. Thomas Malthus claimed that disease, war, famine, and _____ act as checks on population growth.

   (A) moral restraining
   (B) morally restrain
   (C) by moral restraint
   (D) moral restraint

14. _____ phobias do not involve loss of contact with reality, they may severely limit a person's life.

   (A) Although
   (B) Despite
   (C) That
   (D) As

15. During the 1930s, unsuitable farming techniques and excessive grazing of grassland in the Great Plains produced

   _____.

   (A) which it became known as the Dust Bowl
   (B) what became known as the Dust Bowl
   (C) it became known as the Dust Bowl
   (D) that it became known as the Dust Bowl

Directions

The rest of the items in this section consist of sentences in which four words or phrases have been underlined. Choose the one underlined word or phrase that must be changed for the sentence to be correct.

EXAMPLE I

Navajo Indians are far more numerous today as they were in the past.
  A   B   C   D

The best answer is (C). The sentence should read, "Navajo Indians are far more numerous today than they were in the past."

EXAMPLE II

Though it is one of the rarest metals, gold was one of the first to be
  A   B   C

discover.
  D

The best answer is (D). The sentence should read, "Though it is one of the rarest metals, gold was one of the first to be discovered."

16. The first laser is made by an American scientist called Theodore Maiman
    A   B   C
working in California in 1960.
  D

17. Almost medical doctors have had some training in psychology and
    A   B   C   D
psychiatry.

18. Washington Irving, one of America's most famous authors, was a lawyer,
                                          A   B
a businessman, and a United States diplomatic to England and Spain.
                    C   D

19. The Douglas fir is a very tall American evergreen tree that is grown not
                                                              A
only for ornament and for its high-quality timber.
          B   C   D

20. Nuclear energy, <u>a</u> almost <u>limitless</u> source of power, <u>was harnessed</u>
                 A   B   C
    during the <u>mid-1900s</u>.
                  D

21. Plants, which <u>make up</u> 90 <u>percentage</u> of visible <u>living</u> organisms, get
                  A   B   C
    their <u>food</u> energy from sunlight.
        D

22. <u>Total</u> eclipses of the moon <u>are</u> <u>considerably</u> <u>rarest</u> than total eclipses of
     A   B   C   D
    the sun.

23. <u>According to</u> Freud, mental life is <u>characterized</u> by internal conflicts <u>who</u>
         A   B   C
    are <u>largely</u> unconscious.
        D

24. In 1729, Benjamin Franklin <u>published</u> the *Pennsylvania Gazette,* <u>which</u>
                                 A   D
    <u>soon</u> became the most <u>read widely</u> newspaper in the colonies.
     C   D

25. Large, <u>perfect</u> shaped pearls rank <u>in</u> value with <u>the</u> most <u>precious</u>
            A   B   C   D
    stones.

26. Algae range <u>in</u> size from <u>microscope</u> <u>one-celled</u> plants to huge <u>masses</u> of
             A   B   C   D
    seaweed.

27. <u>The</u> pharmacology is a recent science, but it is <u>closely</u> connected with
     A   B
    one of the oldest, <u>the</u> giving of <u>remedies</u> to relieve diseases.
                     C   D

28. Frances Perkins, <u>the</u> first woman to become <u>a</u> U.S. cabinet member, was
                  A   B
    <u>instrument</u> in the <u>adoption</u> of the Social Security Act.
      C   D

29. In the <u>company</u> of human beings, parrots demonstrate a <u>remarkable</u>
            A   B
    talent <u>for</u> mimicry, <u>for which</u> they never use in the forest.
         C   D

30. <u>The</u> first <u>national</u> known male singers <u>of</u> popular music <u>appeared</u> during
     A   B   C   D
    the 1920s.

31. The Puffer is <u>a</u> type of fish <u>that</u> can inflate <u>one's</u> body <u>like</u> a balloon.
             A   B   C   D

32. The <u>Louisiana Purchase</u>, made in 1803, <u>almost</u> <u>was doubled</u> <u>the</u> size of
               A   B   C   D
    the United States.

33. Psychology did not develop <u>into</u> a science <u>based of</u> <u>careful</u> observation
                              A   B   C
    and <u>experimentation</u> until the late 1800s.
         D

34. <u>When</u> a mineral forms, it grows <u>by</u> the addition of various <u>element</u> to <u>its</u>
     A   B   C   D
    structure.

35. Energy exists <u>in</u> different <u>forms</u>, such as light, heat, and chemical,
               A   B
    <u>mechanic</u>, and <u>electrical</u> energy.
       C   D

36. Modern art began in <u>second</u> half of <u>the</u> 1800s, <u>after</u> the camera <u>was</u>
                      A   B   C   D
    invented.

37. <u>Although</u> polar bears hunt <u>other</u> animals, they <u>seldom</u> rarely <u>kill</u> people.
      A   B   C   D

38. Mushrooms get <u>their</u> food <u>by</u> causing <u>vegetable</u> matter <u>decaying</u>.
              A   B   C   D

39. Limestone has <u>long</u> been quarried <u>for</u> <u>to use</u> <u>as</u> a <u>building</u> stone.
             A   B C   D

40. The newborn marsupial is <u>at</u> a <u>least</u> developed stage of life <u>than</u> a
                       A   B   C
    newborn kitten <u>or</u> human being.
            D

PRACTICE TEST 2

Answers on page 196

Directions

Items in the first part of this section are incomplete sentences. Under each of these sentences, there are four words or phrases. Choose the one word or phrase that best completes the sentence.

EXAMPLE I

Reflexes _____ very valuable in protecting the body against harm.

(A) that are
(B) being
(C) are
(D) are being

The best answer is (C). The sentence should read, "Reflexes are very valuable in protecting the body against harm."

EXAMPLE II

Seismographs are used to locate oil, to determine ocean depth, and _____ and measure earthquakes.

(A) detect
(B) to detect
(C) be detecting
(D) are detecting

The best answer is (B). The sentence should read, "Seismographs are used to locate oil, to determine ocean depth, and to detect and measure earthquakes."

---

1. The core of the moon is much smaller, in relation to its size, _____ of the planets
   - (A) those
   - (B) than those
   - (C) ones
   - (D) than is those

2. Silver is sometimes mixed with copper _____ an alloy that is harder and stronger than pure silver.
   - (A) to form
   - (B) forms
   - (C) it forms
   - (D) the forming of

3. Samuel Clemens, _____ under the pen name Mark Twain, created characters that reflected purely American traits and habits.
   - (A) he wrote
   - (B) and he wrote
   - (C) who wrote
   - (D) wrote

4. _____ beetles have hard wing cases that protect the wings when not in use.
   - (A) Of all
   - (B) All
   - (C) Because all
   - (D) They are all

5. Not _____ anywhere in the thirteen colonies before the American Revolution.
   - (A) a single bank
   - (B) a bank existed single
   - (C) existed a single bank
   - (D) a single bank existed

6. _____ mosquito bites a human being or other animal suffering from a certain disease, it carries off the disease germs in its saliva.
   - (A) A
   - (B) Should a
   - (C) Whenever a
   - (D) That a

7. _____ in 1607, Jamestown in Virginia was the first settlement in the New World.
   - (A) Founded
   - (B) It was founded
   - (C) Founding
   - (D) To be found

8. Both the lantern fish and the deep sea angler _____ a luminous gland system in their bodies.
   - (A) they have
   - (B) have
   - (C) had
   - (D) having

9. An effective paragraph must _____ be unified and ordered but also complete.
   - (A) in addition
   - (B) either
   - (C) not only
   - (D) as well

10. _____, the Mormons fled from Illinois in 1846.
    - (A) Their religious beliefs made
    - (B) Their religious beliefs because
    - (C) Because their beliefs, religious
    - (D) Because of their religious beliefs

11. Aristotle, _____ the greatest of the Greek philosophers, wrote extensively about physics and other sciences.

    (A)   one of
    (B)   he is one of
    (C)   of
    (D)   it is he one of

12. Exactly _____ we can replace our soil disappearing through erosion is not known.

    (A)   what
    (B)   how
    (C)   if
    (D)   by which

13. _____ varieties of potato that produce three-quarters of the U.S. potato crop.

    (A)   There are four
    (B)   They are four
    (C)   Four of the
    (D)   Of the four

14. Henry Ford, _____, was an outstanding innovator.

    (A)   he founded the Ford Motor Company
    (B)   founded the Ford Motor Company
    (C)   who founded the Ford Motor Company
    (D)   the Ford Motor Company founded

15. Pheasants spend most of their time on the ground, _____ many species perch in trees at night.

    (A)   as well as
    (B)   in spite of
    (C)   because
    (D)   although

Directions

The rest of the items in this section consist of sentences in which four words or phrases have been underlined. You must identify the **one** underlined expression—(A), (B), (C), or (D)—that must be changed in order to correct the sentence.

EXAMPLE I

Navajo Indians are far more numerous today as they were in the past.
    A   B   C   D

The best answer is (C). The sentence should read, "Navajo Indians are far more numerous today than they were in the past."

EXAMPLE II

Though it is one of the rarest metals, gold was one of the first to be discover.
  A   B   C   D

The best answer is (D). The sentence should read, "Though it is one of the rarest metals, gold was one of the first to be discovered."

---

16. Wind erodes the land by picking up grains of sand and hurling it against
    A   B   C   D
rocks.

17. The Kodak was the first camera designed specifically for both mass
              A   B   C
production or amateur use.
         D

18. Phlebitis, an inflammation of a vein, can develop in any part of the body,
                        A   B
but it most commonly occurs in their legs.
        C   D

19. Certain bacteria can capture light energy and uses it to make food.
       A   B   C   D

20. During the 1850s and 1860s many people began to experiment with the
    A B   C
artist possibilities of photography.
  D

---

21. Aristotle believed that <u>the mind</u> or soul, <u>who</u> the Greeks called psyche,
       A   B
<u>was separate</u> from <u>the body</u>.
       C   D

22. The earth is <u>the</u> only planet with a large <u>number</u> of <u>oxygen</u> in <u>its</u>
                   A   B   C   D
atmosphere.

23. <u>The</u> exciting, <u>naturally</u>, free movement of <u>modern dance</u> <u>began</u> with
     A   B   C   D
Isadora Duncan.

24. Albany, <u>a</u> city on <u>the</u> Hudson River, <u>is</u> <u>the</u> capital of New York State
            A   B   C   D
since 1797.

25. <u>Birds</u> have <u>a poor</u> sense of <u>smell</u> but very good <u>hearings</u> and eyesight.
     A   B   C   D

26. Placebos <u>look like</u> real <u>drugs</u>, <u>but</u> most consist only <u>in</u> sugar or a salt
              A   B   C   D
solution.

27. The Pueblo Indians have <u>traditionally</u> <u>live</u> in stone or adobe <u>structures</u>
                             A   B   C
<u>that</u> resemble apartment buildings.
 D

28. Fabrics woven <u>from</u> plastic fibers feel <u>soft</u>, but the fibers <u>are make</u> from
                   A   B   C
hard <u>plastics</u>.
      D

29. <u>In about 1960</u>, <u>chemists</u> have developed synthetic pheromones <u>that</u> are
     A   B   C
used to control <u>insect pests</u>.
                  D

30. The spinal cord is <u>the</u> main pathway <u>for</u> messages <u>traveling</u> between the
                        A   B   C
brain <u>to</u> the rest of the body.
       D

31. After Yellowstone National Park <u>was set up</u> in 1871 <u>as</u> the first National
                                     A   B
Park, <u>another</u> national parks have been established <u>throughout</u> the
       C   D
world.

32. Nearly all chemical agents <u>are harmful to</u> living tissue if enough of <u>them</u>
    <u>A</u>   B   C
    <u>is taken</u>.
    D

33. In 1875, the American philosopher William James <u>founded</u> <u>what</u> was
                                                    A   B

    <u>probable</u> the world's first <u>psychology</u> laboratory.
    C   D

34. Few natural prairie regions <u>remain</u> in the world <u>because of</u> most of <u>them</u>
                                A   B   C
    have been turned <u>into</u> farms or grazing land.
                     D

35. Most species of <u>pigeons</u> <u>live</u> in flocks, and many of the flocks <u>consist</u>
                    A   B   C
    more than <u>one species</u>.
              D

36. <u>Astronomers</u> do not <u>think</u> <u>are there</u> <u>any</u> planets in the solar system
    A   B   C   D
    beyond Pluto.

37. When an enemy <u>scares</u> a porcupine fish, it enters <u>a hole</u> in a rock and
                  A   B
    to <u>fill</u> its stomach with water to make <u>its</u> spines stick out.
       C   D

38. Robert Frost was not well known <u>as</u> <u>a poet</u> until he <u>reached</u> <u>the</u> forties.
                                    A   B   C   D

39. Mushrooms <u>get</u> their <u>food</u> by <u>to cause</u> vegetable <u>matter</u> to decay.
              A   B   C   D

40. The pharynx plays an important <u>significant</u> role in speech, <u>especially</u> <u>in</u>
    A   B   C   D
    the production of vowel sounds.

PRACTICE TEST 3

Answers on page 196

Directions

Items in the first part of this section are incomplete sentences. Under each of these sentences, there are four words or phrases. Choose the one word or phrase that best completes the sentence.

EXAMPLE I

Reflexes _____ very valuable in protecting the body against harm.

- (A) that are
- (B) being
- (C) are
- (D) are being

The best answer is (C). The sentence should read, "Reflexes are very valuable in protecting the body against harm."

EXAMPLE II

Seismographs are used to locate oil, to determine ocean depth, and _____ and measure earthquakes.

- (A) detect
- (B) to detect
- (C) be detecting
- (D) are detecting

The best answer is (B). The sentence should read, "Seismographs are used to locate oil, to determine ocean depth, and to detect and measure earthquakes."

1. Dow Jones and Company, _____, computes averages for each trading hour of every business day.

   (A) a financial publishing firm
   (B) is a financial publishing firm
   (C) that is a financial publishing firm
   (D) it is a financial publishing firm

2. _____ pipelines are expensive to build, they are relatively cheap to operate and maintain.

   (A) Because
   (B) That
   (C) Although
   (D) Despite

3. The pulse rate of children is faster _____ healthy adult.

   (A) the average
   (B) than that of the average
   (C) that of the average
   (D) as that of the average

4. During the 1970s, Thomas G. Stockham, Jr., a U.S. electrical engineer, _____ digital recording.

   (A) he developed
   (B) that developed
   (C) that he has developed
   (D) developed

5. In 1850 _____ established one of the first detective agencies in the United States.

   (A) detective Allan Pinkerton
   (B) it was detective Allan Pinkerton
   (C) detective Allan Pinkerton who
   (D) when detective Allan Pinkerton

6. _____, scientists have greatly increased the yield of crops such as corn, rice, and wheat.

   (A) As using the laws of genetics
   (B) Using the laws of genetics
   (C) The laws of genetics
   (D) The laws of genetics are to be used

7. _____, and they are separated from one another by vast distances.

   (A) Being millions of galaxies
   (B) Are millions of galaxies
   (C) Of the millions of galaxies
   (D) There are millions of galaxies

8. In 1776, Thomas Paine's popular and influential pamphlet *Common Sense* _____ the American colonists to declare their independence from English rule.

   (A) urged
   (B) to urge
   (C) to be urged
   (D) that urged

9. Artificial satellites provide data on atmospheric temperatures, solar radiation, and _____ the earth's surface.

   (A) reflect
   (B) reflecting
   (C) the reflection of
   (D) can reflect

10. The United States leads the world in the production of plastics, _____ about half the total output.

(A) it supplies
(B) supplying
(C) to supply
(D) supplies

11. _____ affect a person's body has long been known by doctors.

(A) That emotional disturbances
(B) Emotional disturbances
(C) As emotional disturbances
(D) If emotional disturbances

12. Regarded as one of the greatest physicists, _____.

(A) the relationship between force and motion was first expressed by Isaac Newton
(B) the first to express the relationship between force and motion was Isaac Newton
(C) Isaac Newton was the first to express the relationship between force and motion
(D) it was Isaac Newton who was the first to express the relationship between force and motion

13. When direct-dial telephones achieved _____ in the 1960s, nationwide faxing became possible.

(A) used widespread
(B) were used widespread
(C) being used widespread
(D) widespread use

14. Willa Cather, _____ a prominent American writer, grew up in Nebraska during the early farming years.

(A) who became
(B) became
(C) she became
(D) it is she who became

15. _____ few species that live on the ground, most monkeys live in trees.

(A) There are
(B) A
(C) All but
(D) Except for a

Directions

The rest of the items in this section consist of sentences in which four words or phrases have been underlined. Choose the one underlined word or phrase that must be changed for the sentence to be correct.

EXAMPLE I

Navajo Indians are far more numerous today as they were in the past.
   A   B   C   D

The sentence should read, "Navajo Indians are far more numerous today than they were in the past." You should therefore choose answer (C).

EXAMPLE II

Though it is one of the rarest metals, gold was one of the first to be discover.
   A   B   C   D

The sentence should read, "Though it is one of the rarest metals, gold was one of the first to be discovered." You should therefore choose answer (D).

16. A Geiger counter is an electronic instrument is used to measure the
    A   B   C
    presence and intensity of radiation.
                    D

17. Warning coloration protects a skunk by reminding the animal's enemies
    A   B
    of their ability to spray a foul-smelling liquid.
       C   D

18. Natural gas was probably formed from plants and animals that decayed
                        A   B   C
    million of years ago.
       D

19. Three months after they have been laid, crocodile eggs are ready
                                      A   B   C
    hatched.
       D

20. The terrain of Antarctica, near one and a half times as big as the United
                              A   B   C
    States, is amazingly varied.
                    D

21. Peas require <u>rich</u> soil, constant <u>moistures</u>, and a cool <u>growing</u> season to
           A   B   C
    develop <u>well</u>.
           D

22. The <u>amount</u> of pectin <u>in</u> a fruit <u>depends</u> the species and <u>ripeness</u>.
          A   B   C   D

23. <u>Most</u> pageants are plays of special <u>significant</u> such as <u>a</u> drama <u>portraying</u>
      A   B   C   D
    the growth of a city or the development of medicine.

24. Joseph Priestley is <u>immortal</u> in the <u>history</u> of <u>chemistry</u> as the <u>discover</u>
                        A   B   C   D
    of oxygen, in 1774.

25. Mosses are useful <u>in</u> nature <u>because of</u> they are <u>among</u> <u>the</u> first plants to
                  A   B   C   D
    grow in barren lands.

26. <u>Dreaming</u> sleep may play a role <u>in</u> restoring the brain's ability to handle
      A   B
    such tasks as <u>focused</u> attention, <u>memorize</u>, and learning.
                 C   D

27. <u>The most</u> desert animals <u>avoid</u> the extreme midday <u>heat</u> by <u>feeding</u> at
        A   B   C   D
    night.

28. <u>Although</u> <u>fewer</u> Americans work on farms today, they are <u>too</u> productive
      A   B   C
    that the U.S. is now the world's <u>top</u> food exporter.
                             D

29. Seals, turtles, and seabirds can navigate <u>over</u> <u>thousands</u> of miles of open
                                       A   B
    ocean with <u>amazing</u> <u>accurate</u>.
                 C   D

30. Most mollusks have <u>a</u> hard <u>shell</u> <u>that</u> is <u>protected</u> their soft bodies.
                     A   B   C   D

31. Foods of animal origin generally <u>supply</u> <u>greatest</u> <u>amounts</u> of iron to <u>the</u>
                                A   B   C   D
    diet than do foods of plant origin.

32. A dolphin locates underwater objects <u>in</u> <u>its</u> path by <u>doing</u> a series of
                                     A B   C

    clicking and <u>whistling</u> sounds.
                D

33. <u>In 1829</u>, James Smithson <u>set aside</u> money for <u>creating</u> of <u>the</u> Smithsonian
       A   B   C   D
    Institute.

34. <u>A</u> pheromone is a chemical substance released by <u>many</u> kinds of animals
    A   B
    to communicate with <u>another</u> members of <u>their</u> species.
                      C   D

35. The skin receives <u>nearly</u> <u>the</u> third of the blood <u>pumped out</u> <u>by</u> the heart.
                      A   B   C   D

36. <u>Alike</u> <u>most</u> small bats that fly by night, the large flying foxes <u>fly</u> <u>by</u> day.
      A   B   C D

37. Recognition <u>for</u> Herman Melville <u>did not come</u> <u>until</u> more than thirty
                 A   B   C
    years <u>afterward</u> his death in 1891.
           D

38. The Dewey system <u>is</u> widely used by libraries <u>throughout</u> the world; the
                    A   B
    <u>classification</u> <u>be</u> constantly revised.
         C   D

39. Ten <u>percent</u> of blood plasma is made up <u>mainly</u> <u>of</u> blood proteins,
        A   B C
    which enable <u>itself</u> to clot.
               D

40. The American <u>frontiersman</u>, politician, and soldier Davy Crockett is one
                 A

    of the <u>most</u> popular <u>of</u> American <u>hero</u>.
         B   C   D

PRACTICE TEST 4

Answers on page 197

Directions

Items in the first part of this section are incomplete sentences. Under each of these sentences, there are four words or phrases. Choose the one word or phrase that best completes the sentence.

EXAMPLE I

Reflexes _____ very valuable in protecting the body against harm.

   (A) that are
   (B) being
   (C) are
   (D) are being

The best answer is (C). The sentence should read, "Reflexes are very valuable in protecting the body against harm."

EXAMPLE II

Seismographs are used to locate oil, to determine ocean depth, and _____ and measure earthquakes.

   (A) detect
   (B) to detect
   (C) be detecting
   (D) are detecting

The best answer is (B). The sentence should read, "Seismographs are used to locate oil, to determine ocean depth, and to detect and measure earthquakes."

---

1. Blood in vessels just under the nasal lining _____ up its heat to warm the air.

   (A) gives
   (B) it gives
   (C) giving
   (D) is given

2. The shuttle, _____ reusable spacecraft, lifts off like a rocket and lands like an airplane.

   (A) it is a
   (B) a
   (C) which, as a
   (D) is a

3. _____ forms of life, the most varied are the insects.

   (A) All are
   (B) All
   (C) They are all
   (D) Of all

4. The first American _____ a professional sculptor was a woman, Patience Lovell Wright.

   (A) she became as
   (B) became
   (C) to become
   (D) who she became

5. Tears not only _____ foreign substances from the eyes, but they also contain chemicals that fight many common pathogens.

   (A) for washing
   (B) are washing
   (C) washing
   (D) wash

6. Carbonated beverages became popular in 1832 after _____ an apparatus for charging water with carbon dioxide gas.

   (A) invented John Mathews
   (B) John Mathews invented
   (C) inventing John Mathews
   (D) John Mathews inventing

7. The Pawnee Indians regarded corn _____ sacred gift, and many of their religious ceremonies are centered around this crop.

   (A) as being
   (B) since a
   (C) as a
   (D) like being

8. On Jupiter the winds have created storms _____ big that astronomers on Earth can see them through their telescopes.

   (A) so
   (B) such
   (C) as
   (D) how

9. Larger animals _____ than smaller animals of the same type.

   (A) longer live generally
   (B) they generally live long
   (C) generally live longer
   (D) live generally long

10. The tails of comets generally point away from the sun _____ the comet is approaching the sun or receding.

    (A) either
    (B) whether
    (C) and if
    (D) both

11. A desert is described as a region _____ an average of less than ten inches of rain falls in a year.

    (A) there is
    (B) which has
    (C) in which is
    (D) in which

12. Regular radio broadcasting to inform and entertain the general public _____ in the 1920s.

    (A) started
    (B) starting
    (C) a start
    (D) to start

13. _____ was made of minute particles called corpuscles was believed by scientists.

    (A) Light
    (B) That light
    (C) As light
    (D) Whereas light

14. _____ rain at all falls in the dry season in the savanna regions of Africa.

    (A) Not
    (B) Without
    (C) No
    (D) Neither

15. In a Rorschach test, the subject describes _____ sees in a series of inkblots.

    (A) that he or she
    (B) he or she
    (C) seeing he or she
    (D) what he or she

Directions

The rest of the items in this section consist of sentences in which four words or phrases have been underlined. Choose the one underlined word or phrase that must be changed for the sentence to be correct.

EXAMPLE I

$$\underset{A}{\underline{\text{Navajo Indians}}} \text{ are } \underset{B}{\underline{\text{far}}} \text{ more numerous today } \underset{C}{\underline{\text{as}}} \text{ they were } \underset{D}{\underline{\text{in}}} \text{ the past.}$$

The best answer is (C). The sentence should read, "Navajo Indians are far more numerous today than they were in the past."

EXAMPLE II

$$\underset{A}{\underline{\text{Though}}} \text{ it is one of the rarest } \underset{B}{\underline{\text{metals}}}, \text{ gold was one of } \underset{C}{\underline{\text{the}}} \text{ first to be}$$

$$\underset{D}{\underline{\text{discover}}}.$$

The best answer is (D). The sentence should read, "Though it is one of the rarest metals, gold was one of the first to be discovered."

---

16. Pigeons, $\underset{A}{\underline{\text{like}}}$ many migratory birds, $\underset{B}{\underline{\text{read}}}$ the positions of

$\underset{C}{\underline{\text{the sun and stars}}}$ in order to orient $\underset{D}{\underline{\text{them}}}$.

17. The $\underset{A}{\underline{\text{cracking}}}$ of rocks is caused $\underset{B}{\underline{\text{of}}}$ intense heat during the day followed

$\underset{C}{\underline{\text{by}}}$ rapid $\underset{D}{\underline{\text{cooling}}}$ at night.

18. Our nervous system has over ten $\underset{A}{\underline{\text{billions}}}$ $\underset{B}{\underline{\text{nerve}}}$ cells in a network

covering $\underset{C}{\underline{\text{every}}}$ inch of our skin and $\underset{D}{\underline{\text{organs}}}$.

19. Great $\underset{A}{\underline{\text{quantities}}}$ of $\underset{B}{\underline{\text{the}}}$ $\underset{C}{\underline{\text{seaweed}}}$ are found in $\underset{D}{\underline{\text{the}}}$ Sargasso Sea.

20. $\underset{A}{\underline{\text{Giant}}}$ tortoises live $\underset{B}{\underline{\text{to}}}$ great ages, and specimens have been known

$\underset{C}{\underline{\text{to live}}}$ from 100 $\underset{D}{\underline{\text{and}}}$ 150 years.

21. Fermentation, the <u>breaking down</u> of simple sugars, produces either
    A
    <u>lactic acid</u> <u>or</u> <u>ethyl</u> alcoholic and carbon dioxide.
      B   C   D

22. <u>Most</u> pines grow <u>rapidly</u> and form straight, tall trunks <u>that</u> are <u>ideally</u> for
      A   B   C   D
    lumber.

23. By <u>measuring</u> <u>the</u> color of a star, astronomers can tell <u>how</u> hot <u>is it</u>.
         A   B   C   D

24. <u>Many</u> fruits contain large <u>amounts</u> of vitamin C, <u>as well as</u> sugar, which
      A   B   C
    <u>provide</u> energy.
      D

25. <u>Valuable</u> pearls come from some species of oysters and <u>another</u> mollusks
      A   B
    <u>that</u> live in tropical <u>seas</u>.
      C   D

26. <u>Freud's ideas</u> have <u>had</u> a great influence <u>on</u> the study of personality, but
      A   B   C
    they are <u>highly controversy</u>.
            D

27. The Dodge brothers began <u>doing</u> their own automobiles in 1914 and
                            A
    produced <u>one of</u> the first American <u>automobiles</u> with an <u>all-steel</u> body.
            B   C   D

28. <u>Children's</u> ears are able <u>to detect</u> a <u>wide</u> variety of <u>pitches</u> than those of
      A   B   C   D
    adults.

29. *Euglena* is a <u>single-celled</u> organism that has <u>characteristic</u> <u>of</u> <u>both</u> plants
                 A   B   C   D
    and animals.

30. <u>Morse</u> code was <u>an</u> important way to send <u>messages</u> before the tele-
      A   B   C
    phone and radio <u>are</u> invented.
                  D

31. Many plains, <u>such</u> the Great Plains in the United States, have <u>few</u> trees
               A   B
    because <u>of</u> dry or cold <u>climates</u>.
           C   D

32. <u>Much</u> psychologists do not associate <u>themselves</u> <u>with</u> a <u>particular</u> school
      A   B   C   D
    or theory.

33. Prussic acid is one of the <u>most</u> poisonous <u>substances</u> <u>known</u>, <u>neither</u> as
                              A   B   C   D
    a liquid or a gas.

34. Compact discs, <u>which</u> appeared on the market in the early 1980s,
                A
    <u>produce</u> sound of better quality than <u>those</u> of standard <u>phonograph</u>
      B   C   D
    records.

35. The Pony Express began at a time <u>when</u> <u>not</u> railway went <u>farther</u> west
                                   A   B   C
    <u>than</u> the Mississippi and Missouri rivers.
     D

36. The Homestead Act of 1862 granted 160 acres of land to <u>any</u> settler
                                                    A
    <u>which</u> <u>would</u> spend five years <u>on</u> the land.
      B   C   D

37. Dust storms occur <u>however</u> wind erosion is <u>strong</u> and loose <u>material</u> <u>is</u>
                     A   B   C   D
    exposed.

38. Pewter <u>ranks</u> as one of the oldest <u>known</u> alloys and may <u>have</u> been used
          A   B   C
    as early as 1500 B.C. <u>ago</u>.
                    D

39. <u>Warm</u> and moisture help microbes <u>grow</u> and <u>thus</u> assist the <u>decay</u>
     A   B   C   D
    process.

40. Parrots are noisy, <u>sociable</u> birds that live <u>mainly</u> chiefly in forested areas
       A   B   C
    <u>in</u> lowlands and mountains.
     D

PRACTICE TEST 5

Answers on page 197

Directions

Items in the first part of this section are incomplete sentences. Under each of these sentences, there are four words or phrases. Choose the one word or phrase that best completes the sentence.

EXAMPLE I

Reflexes _____ very valuable in protecting the body against harm.

(A) that are
(B) being
(C) are
(D) are being

The best answer is (C). The sentence should read, "Reflexes are very valuable in protecting the body against harm."

EXAMPLE II

Seismographs are used to locate oil, to determine ocean depth, and _____ and measure earthquakes.

(A) detect
(B) to detect
(C) be detecting
(D) are detecting

The best answer is (B). The sentence should read, "Seismographs are used to locate oil, to determine ocean depth, and to detect and measure earthquakes."

1. The behavior of many volcanoes _____ very difficult to predict, especially the more explosive types.
   - (A) are
   - (B) is
   - (C) that
   - (D) being

2. _____ more than 2,000 minerals are known, nearly all rocks are formed from seven mineral groups.
   - (A) Although
   - (B) However
   - (C) Despite
   - (D) Since

3. Alexander Graham Bell worked with deaf students before _____ the first telephone in 1876.
   - (A) designed
   - (B) was designed
   - (C) to design
   - (D) designing

4. An enzyme works by coming in contact with a particular substance, _____ with it, and changing it.
   - (A) combines
   - (B) combining
   - (C) it combines
   - (D) to combine

5. Foods of animal origin generally supply greater amounts of iron to the diet than _____.
   - (A) are foods of plant origin
   - (B) foods of plant origins
   - (C) do foods of plant origin
   - (D) plant origin foods

6. _____ energy for growth or repair, a plant must carry out photosynthesis.
   - (A) To obtain
   - (B) It obtains
   - (C) It is obtaining
   - (D) Obtaining

7. Nicotine, _____ found in tobacco, is named after the French diplomat Jean Nicot.
   - (A) it is a chemical compound
   - (B) is a chemical compound
   - (C) a chemical compound
   - (D) chemical compound is

8. _____ the world's most successful artificial language.
   - (A) As Esperanto is
   - (B) That Esperanto
   - (C) It is Esperanto
   - (D) Esperanto is

9. _____ food we eat lacks minerals, then the body can use the stores from its bones for more urgent needs.
   - (A) As the
   - (B) If the
   - (C) The
   - (D) Since

10. _____ an organism to become a fossil.
    - (A) Rarely
    - (B) It is rare
    - (C) Rare is
    - (D) It is rare for

11. Among sea horses, _____ carries and hatches the eggs in a special breeding pouch.
    - (A) it is the male that
    - (B) the male it
    - (C) it is the male
    - (D) the male who

12. _____ will be increasingly used as a source of petrochemicals when oil begins to run out.

   (A) No matter coal
   (B) No doubt coal
   (C) If coal
   (D) That coal

13. Scientists have discovered that the jellylike material in cells _____ proteins and other substances.

   (A) is actually a complex mixture
   (B) it is actually a complex mixture
   (C) actually is a complex mixture of
   (D) that actually are a complex mixture of

14. The discovery that electricity could produce magnetism _____ in 1820 by the Danish physicist, Hans Christian Oersted.

   (A) by accident
   (B) was an accident
   (C) was made by accident
   (D) by accident was

15. Digital systems work first by changing quantity and then _____ into strips of numbers.

   (A) convert the measurements
   (B) the measurements convert
   (C) to convert the measurements
   (D) converting the measurements

Directions

The rest of the items in this section consist of sentences in which four words or phrases have been underlined. Choose the one underlined word or phrase that must be changed for the sentence to be correct.

EXAMPLE I

Navajo Indians are far more numerous today as they were in the past.
    A   B   C   D

The best answer is (C). The sentence should read, "Navajo Indians are far more numerous today than they were in the past."

EXAMPLE II

Though it is one of the rarest metals, gold was one of the first to be discover.
  A   B   C   D

The best answer is (D). The sentence should read, "Though it is one of the rarest metals, gold was one of the first to be discovered."

---

16. National forests including land for animal grazing, as well as wilderness
                  A   B   C
    areas with scenic mountains and lakes.
          D

17. The Pony Express from 1860 to 1861 became one of the most colorful
                                A   B
    episodes in American post history.
    C   D

18. Contact lenses made of acrylic are more transparent and least fragile
                              A   B
    than lenses made of glass.
   C   D

19. There is no oxygen in space to support the combustion of fuels as
         A   B
    is there in the air on Earth.
     C   D

20. As early as 4000 B.C., people used irons from meteorites to make
                          A   B
    ornaments, weapons, tools and utensils.
   C   D

21. The pioneers <u>raised</u> corn as <u>their</u> chief crop because <u>they</u> kept well in
           A   B   C
    any season and <u>could be</u> used in many ways.
                        D

22. A coral reef consists <u>in millions</u> of tiny coral polyps, which are <u>a</u> form of
                              A   B
    small <u>animal</u> <u>related to</u> anemones and jellyfishes.
            C   D

23. In <u>an</u> ordinary <u>optical</u> microscope, <u>a</u> electric bulb or sunlight is used as
         A   B   C
    <u>light</u> for the stage.
      D

24. Eleanor Roosevelt had <u>long a</u> career of public service as a <u>champion</u> of
                              A   B
    <u>human</u> rights, a writer, and a <u>delegate</u> to the United Nations.
      C   D

25. Psychologists use <u>standardized</u> tests to help <u>measure</u> abilities, aptitudes,
                          A   B
    <u>interesting</u>, and <u>personality</u> traits.
        C   D

26. Meriwether Lewis and William Clark <u>were commissioned</u> <u>by</u> the U.S.
                                              A   B
    government to map the <u>lands</u> between St. Louis <u>to</u> the Pacific.
                              C   D

27. <u>As</u> a pure white sugar, dextrose <u>used</u> mainly <u>in</u> candy, baked goods, and
     A   B   C
    <u>canned</u> goods.
      D

28. Paul Dunbar wrote poetry in <u>standard</u> English about <u>tradition</u> poetic
                                    A   B
    subjects and about <u>the</u> <u>heroes</u> of black Americans.
                          C   D

29. It is estimated that <u>at least</u> a <u>million</u> meteors <u>have hit</u> the Earth's land
                            A   B   C
    surface, which is only 25 <u>percentage</u> of the planet.
                                  D

30. The pituitary gland is a small endocrine gland <u>at</u> the base of the brain
                                                      A
    that releases <u>many</u> hormones and <u>regulates</u> <u>another</u> endocrine glands.
                      B   C   D

31. A persimmon tastes <u>best</u> when it is <u>such</u> ripe that it looks <u>wrinkled</u> and
                            A   B   C
    <u>almost</u> spoiled.
      D

32. American pioneers <u>did</u> water systems from logs with holes <u>bored</u>
                  A   B
    through <u>their</u> <u>centers</u>.
              C   D

33. Polls <u>following</u> <u>scientific</u> procedures began in 1935 with the <u>experiment</u>
           A   B   C
    nationwide <u>surveys</u> of George Gallup and Elm Roper.
               D

34. In America, the Indians used crude oil for <u>fuel</u> and medicine <u>hundreds</u> of
                                            A   B
    years <u>before</u> the first white settlers <u>arrive</u>.
            C   D

35. When radio programs <u>became</u> popular, <u>approximately</u> around 1925,
      A   B   C
    many people stopped <u>attending</u> movies.
                         D

36. Musical comedies, <u>as</u> an American form of <u>entertainment</u>, often take <u>its</u>
                   A   B   C
    subjects from America's present <u>or</u> past.
                       D

37. <u>Of</u> all seashore plants, seaweeds are <u>best</u> able to tolerate long periods
    A   B
    out of water, followed <u>by</u> long periods <u>covering</u> by water.
                      C   D

38. The fruit of the plantain looks <u>much</u> like a banana, <u>and</u> it is not so sweet
                                  A   B
    or so <u>pleasing</u> in <u>flavor</u>.
           C   D

39. The viceroy butterfly, an insect <u>that</u> birds like to eat, has a color pattern
                                    A
    similar <u>to</u> that <u>of</u> the monarch butterfly, <u>whom</u> birds do not like to eat.
           B   C   D

40. Behavior therapy uses rewards and <u>punishments</u> to encourage patients
                                    A
    to act <u>in</u> a <u>way</u> <u>healthier</u>.
      B   C   D

ANSWER KEY

CHAPTER 1

Exercise 1 *(page 3)*
1. information
2. women's
3. one-fourth
4. language, logic
5. art, music
6. pounds
7. pain
8. million nerve

Exercise 2 *(page 3)*
1. F
2. T
3. F
4. T
5. F
6. F

Exercise 3 *(page 6)*
1. Intelligence is the ability to use thought and *knowledge* to understand things and solve problems.
2. Hormones help adjust the mixture of sugar, salt, and *water* in your body.
3. Psychology, the study of the mind and how it works, comes from a Greek word meaning *life* or soul.
4. Brain cells use up a lot of energy, so they need a constant supply of *oxygen*.
5. Each hemisphere of the brain receives *information* about the opposite side of the visual field.
6. Although millions of brain neurons are active at any one time, they do not use much electric *power*.
7. *Light* entering the eye forms an image on 130 million tiny light cells.
8. Most *animals* are not able to rely on learning and memory.

Exercise 4 *(page 7)*
1. People's brains weigh more now than they did 100 *years* ago.
2. *Nerve* impulses can travel at speeds of up to 488 feet per second.
3. The brain contains between 10 *trillion* and 100 *trillion* neurons.
4. Each neuron is linked by synapses to *thousands* of other neurons.
5. *Nerve* endings below the skin's surface pick up sensations of cold, heat, and touch.

6. There are three to four *million* pain receptors in the skin.
7. A three-*year*-old child's brain is two thirds the size it will finally be.
8. The brain uses 25 *percent* of the blood's oxygen.

Exercises on Nouns *(page 9)*
1. D
2. A
3. C
4. A
5. B
6. A
7. A
8. D
9. A
10. C
11. D
12. D

CHAPTER 2

Exercise 1 *(page 12)*
1. They live in Antarctica.
2. She produces one egg.
3. He uses a special fold of skin.
4. They stand together to protect themselves from the cold.
5. They put their eggs on their feet.
6. She goes to find food.
7. She returns after two months.
8. He returns to the sea.

Exercise 2 *(page 13)*
1. T
2. T
3. F
4. F
5. F
6. F
7. T
8. F

Exercise 3 *(page 14)*
1. she
2. He
3. She
4. I
5. He
6. they

Exercise 4 *(page 15)*
1. He helps *her* take care of the baby penguin.
2. Correct
3. Correct
4. It is not easy for *them* to survive under such conditions.
5. It is harder for him than for *her*.
6. Correct

Exercise 5 *(page 16)*
1. her
2. his
3. their
4. its
5. their
6. her

Exercise 6 *(page 17)*
1. his
2. theirs
3. theirs
4. ours
5. hers
6. mine

Exercise 7 *(page 18)*
1. themselves
2. itself
3. herself
4. itself/himself
5. himself
6. ourselves

Exercise 8 *(page 19)*
1. There are eighteen different kinds of penguins *that* live south of the equator.
2. The biologist *who* went to the south pole is studying emperor penguins.
3. Emperor penguins survive winds *that* blow at speeds of up to ninety-five miles an hour in winter.
4. Correct
5. Emperor penguins, *which* are the largest among penguins, do not make nests.
6. The United States has sent researchers to Antarctica *who* are making experiments to measure the energy expended by emperor penguins.

Exercises on Pronouns *(page 21)*
1. B
2. C
3. D
4. D
5. D
6. A
7. A
8. B
9. D
10. C
11. D
12. A

CHAPTER 3
Exercise 1 *(page 23)*
1. At the Boston slave market, Phyllis was purchased by John Wheatley.
2. In a few years, Phyllis had learned geography, history, and Latin.
3. Her mistress, Mrs. Wheatley, was impressed by the child's aptitude.
4. At the age of thirteen, she wrote her first poem.
5. In 1773 her first book of poems was published.
6. With the London publication of her book, her fame spread on both sides of the Atlantic.

Exercise 2 *(page 24)*
1. C
2. NC
3. C
4. NC
5. C
6. C

Exercise 3 *(page 28)*
1. C
2. B
3. A
4. B
5. C
6. D

Exercise 4 *(page 29)*
1. B
2. A
3. D
4. A
5. C

Exercises on Parts of a Sentence
(page 31)
1. A
2. C
3. B
4. D
5. A
6. B
7. D
8. D
9. B
10. D
11. C
12. A

CHAPTER 4
Exercise 1 *(page 33)*
1. comes
2. abolished
3. discovered
4. proposed
5. has been held
6. were
7. were admitted

Exercise 2 *(page 34)*
1. The Olympics *took* place every four years from 776 B.C. to 394 A.D.
2. Correct
3. From 1896 to the present, the Olympic Games *have been held* every four years.
4. Correct
5. With this international competition, Pierre de Coubertin *wanted* to encourage both sport and world peace.
6. In 1916, 1940, and 1944 the Olympic Games *did not* take place.

Exercise 3 *(page 38)*
1. A
2. B
3. C
4. D
5. A
6. B
7. C
8. D

Exercise 4 *(page 40)*
1. was held
2. was built
3. was flown
4. was led
5. were cancelled
6. were shown

Exercise 5 *(page 44)*
1. A
2. B
3. A
4. B
5. B
6. A

Exercises on Verbs *(page 46)*
1. B
2. A
3. C
4. D
5. A
6. B
7. B
8. C
9. B
10. B
11. C
12. C

CHAPTER 5
Exercise 1 *(page 48)*
1. on
2. by
3. In, of
4. by
5. with
6. from, on

Exercise 2 *(page 49)*
1. A potato famine occurred in Ireland in the 1840s. Due to the famine, 1.5 million people died.
2. A flood occurred in Johnstown, Pennsylvania, U.S., in May 1889. Due to the flood, 2200 people died.
3. An earthquake occurred in Tangshan, China, on July 28, 1976. Due to the earthquake, 242,000 people died.
4. A tidal wave occurred in Bangladesh in 1970. Due to the tidal wave, 200,000 people died.
5. A tornado occurred in Ohio, U.S., on April 3, 1974. Due to the tornado, 315 people died.
6. A fire occurred in Yellowstone Park, U.S., in 1980. Due to the fire, 1.3 million acres burned.

Exercise 3 *(page 50)*
1. to
2. from
3. in
4. to
5. by
6. on
7. to
8. on

Exercise 4 *(page 51)*
1. to
2. for
3. of
4. for
5. from
6. to
7. on
8. at

Exercise 5 *(page 52)*
1. of
2. for
3. of
4. of
5. of
6. on
7. of
8. of

Exercise 6 *(page 53)*
1. to
2. to
3. of
4. of
5. of
6. of
7. of
8. to

Exercise 7 *(page 54)*
1. in
2. at, on
3. on
4. In, in
5. in
6. in, in
7. in
8. in, in
9. from, to
10. from, to

Exercise 8 *(page 55)*
1. on
2. At
3. In
4. in
5. on
6. on
7. In
8. by

Exercises on Prepositions *(page 56)*
1. D
2. A
3. C
4. C
5. B
6. D
7. B
8. B
9. D
10. A
11. A
12. B

CHAPTER 6
Exercise 1 *(page 59)*
1. Japan
2. Greenland
3. Australia
4. Great Britain
5. Iceland
6. Surtsey

Exercise 2 *(page 60)*
1. Arctic
2. New Guinea, Pacific
3. Borneo, the, the Pacific
4. Madagascar, the fourth, the Indian
5. Baffin Island, the, the Arctic
6. Sumatra, the sixth, the Indian

Exercise 3 *(page 61)*
1. C
2. NC, a big island
3. C
4. C
5. NC, an uninhabited island
6. C
7. C
8. C
9. NC, and animals

Exercise 4 *(page 64)*
1. the, ø, the
2. The
3. ø, ø, a
4. The, ø, a
5. The, ø, a, ø
6. the, the, ø
7. the, the, ø
8. the, the, ø
9. ø, a, the
10. The, the, the

Exercises on Articles *(page 66)*

1. D
2. B
3. A
4. A
5. D
6. C
7. B
8. B
9. D
10. B
11. A
12. D

CHAPTER 7

Exercise 1 *(page 68)*

1. that
2. that
3. how
4. that/how
5. that
6. that

Exercise 2 *(page 69)*

1. A
2. B
3. A
4. B
5. B

Exercise 3 *(page 71)*

1. NC
2. C
3. C
4. NC
5. NC
6. C

Exercise 4 *(page 72)*

1. C
2. A
3. A
4. B
5. C
6. D

Exercises on Noun Clauses *(page 74)*

1. A
2. B
3. C
4. D
5. A
6. B
7. A
8. D
9. A
10. B
11. B
12. C

CHAPTER 8

Exercise 1 *(page 76)*

1. which
2. whose
3. who
4. which
5. that
6. which

Exercise 2 *(page 77)*

1. which
2. which
3. that
4. which
5. which
6. who

Exercise 3 *(page 78)*

1. Sacagewea. who was a Shoshoni Indian, guided Lewis and Clark to the Columbia River.
2. The giant redwood trees that grow in California, are named after Sequoyah, who created an alphabet for the Indian people.
3. Sequoyah became a teacher and moved to Oklahoma where he continued to teach the alphabet.
4. The Shoshoni were a group of Indians who lived in the western plains of Wyoming, Utah, Nevada, and Idaho.
5. Each group of Shoshoni was known to the others by the type of food that was plentiful in its particular region.
6. The Mossi people of West Africa use talking drums as a means of preserving their history, which has been handed down by generations.

Exercise 4 *(page 80)*

2, 4, 5, 6

Exercise 5 *(page 82)*

1. Sequoyah, the son of an Indian mother and a European father, was born in Tennessee.
2. Sequoyah, first a hunter, became a trader after a hunting accident.
3. Correct
4. Correct
5. His alphabet, consisting of eighty-five sounds, was an important invention for his people.
6. Correct
7. Correct

Exercises on Adjective Clauses (*page 83*)
1. A
2. B
3. C
4. D
5. A
6. B
7. C
8. D
9. B
10. A
11. C
12. D

CHAPTER 9

Exercise 1 (*page 85*)
1. before
2. when
3. when
4. because
5. when
6. although

Exercise 2 (*page 86*)
1. because
2. as
3. where
4. after
5. whereas
6. before

Exercise 3 (*page 88*)
1. Although millions of meteors hit the earth's atmosphere, few of them are noticed.
2. A meteor leaves a bright trail as it streaks across the night sky.
3. Many meteorite falls are not noticed because they hit the earth in remote uninhabited areas.
4. The rate of the sun's radiation is so great that about 3 million tons of matter is converted into energy every second.
5. In ancient times, farmers planted crops when they saw a planet in the right part of the sky.
6. Even though a planet moves among the stars, it returns to the same part of the sky at the same time each year.

Exercise 4 (*page 90*)
1. A
2. B
3. C
4. D
5. B
6. B

Exercises on Adverb Clauses (*page 92*)
1. B
2. B
3. B
4. D
5. C
6. A
7. B
8. D
9. C
10. D
11. B
12. C

CHAPTER 10

Exercise 1 (*page 94*)
1. in, in
2. in, in, of
3. by
4. from, in, in
5. in, by
6. in

Exercise 2 (*page 95*)
1. Richard Long leaves his mark by making changes *in* the landscape.
2. Richard Long brings back found objects *from* his walks.
3. Richard Long uses the objects in sculptures that are shown *in* art galleries.
4. Land art involves the artist going into nature, usually *in* a remote area.
5. The only record that remains of land art is photographic, sometimes combined *with* maps.

Exercise 3 (*page 96*)
1. Artists have painted nature for centuries.
   S   V   O   PP
2. Richard Long recorded his work
   S   V   O
   in different ways.
   PP
3. Most murals are painted
   S   V
   in a naturalistic style.
   PP
4. The role of art in western culture
   S   PP   PP
   has changed in the last hundred years.
   V   PP
5. Futurism emerged in northern Italy
   S   V   PP
   before the First World War.
   PP
6. Some contemporary artists have rejected
   S   V
   art galleries for political reasons.
   O   PP

Exercise 4 *(page 97)*

1. The invention of photography in the 1820s encouraged artists to attempt even greater realism in their paintings.
2. As the 19th century wore on, some artists began to question the need for art to refer to the outside world.
3. By the 19th century, art dealers had begun to sell uncommissioned art to a wider public.
4. Monet was more concerned with expressing an almost mystical sense of communion with nature than with working spontaneously.
5. With the Industrial Revolution the landscape began to change more and more, and artists began to look into its negative and positive aspects.
6. Land art involves the artist going out into nature, usually in a remote area, and making his or her mark on it.

Exercise 5 *(page 97)*

1. A
2. B
3. C
4. D
5. A
6. B
7. C
8. D

Exercises on Prepositional Phrases
(page 99)

1. B
2. A
3. C
4. D
5. A
6. B
7. C
8. D
9. A
10. B
11. C
12. D

CHAPTER 11

Exercise 1 *(page 103)*

1. lesser
2. smallest, highest
3. larger
4. richer
5. brilliant
6. greatest

Exercise 2 *(page 103)*

1. biggest
2. smaller
3. bigger
4. big
5. big
6. smallest

Exercise 3 *(page 107)*

1. highest
2. importantest
3. more older
4. sound the (*as* omitted)
5. low
6. short
7. more
8. the

Exercises on Comparatives and Superlatives *(page 108)*

1. A
2. B
3. C
4. D
5. B
6. A
7. C
8. C
9. B
10. B
11. B
12. C

CHAPTER 12

Exercise 1 *(page 110)*

1. and
2. and
3. and
4. but
5. and
6. and

Exercise 2 *(page 111)*
1. Soya is not only used in many food processes but also in many industrial processes.
2. Soya has been used in the manufacture of paints both for industrial and domestic use.
3. Glycerine is not only used in glues but also in the manufacture of explosives.
4. Soya is used in the manufacture of food both for human consumption and animal consumption.
5. American farmers have been encouraged to grow more soya not only because the export market has expanded but also because the demand at home has increased.
6. The ancient Chinese used the soya bean for both food and medicine.

Exercise 3 *(page 114)*
1. B
2. A
3. C
4. D
5. A
6. B
7. A
8. B

Exercises on Conjunctions *(page 116)*
1. A
2. C
3. D
4. C
5. B
6. B
7. B
8. C
9. D
10. B
11. D
12. D

CHAPTER 13
Exercise 1 *(page 118)*
1. fresh vegetables, fruit
2. gums bled, their skin became rough, their wounds did not heal, their muscles wasted away
3. heat, storage, exposure to air
4. the elderly, alcoholics, the chronically ill
5. speeds would healing, helps prevent gum disease, helps protect us from pollutants such as cigarette smoke.
6. increases life span.

Exercise 2 *(page 119)*
For
1. Lowers cholesterol and fights heart disease.
2. Correct
3. Correct
4. Fights diabetes.
5. Fights gum disease.
6. Strengthens immunity against colds.

Against
1. Wastes money because the body excretes excess vitamin C.
2. Causes kidney stones or gout in some people.
3. Causes diarrhea and stomach cramps in some people.
4. Correct

Exercise 3 *(page 120)*
1. Vitamin E <u>protects against heart disease</u>, <u>prevents cancer</u>, and <u>fights skin problems</u>. (V)
2. The mineral fluoride is found naturally in <u>soils</u>, <u>water</u>, <u>plants</u>, and <u>animal tissue</u>. (N)
3. The tomato plant needs a <u>long growing</u> season and <u>light</u>, <u>rich</u>, <u>well-drained</u> soil. (ADJ)
4. Vitamin E is being employed <u>slowly</u> but <u>steadily</u> in medicine in an expanding range of ailments. (ADV)
5. Studies have shown that vitamin C can reduce <u>the severity and lengths</u> of colds, but not <u>the number of colds a person gets</u>. (N)
6. If you do not have enough iron, you can suffer from anemia, which makes you <u>pale</u>, <u>tired</u>, and <u>weak</u>. (ADJ)

Exercise 4 *(page 121)*
1. Iron-deficiency anemia has been implicated in <u>emotion</u>, social, and learning difficulties in infants, adolescents, and adults.
2. All "B" vitamins are needed for a healthy appetite, energy production in cells, healthy <u>nervous</u>, and skin.
3. Some vitamins may cause toxic, <u>allergy</u> reactions in some people.
4. Symptoms of a mild case of vitamin C deficiency may be weakness, <u>irritable</u>, loss of weight, and apathy.
5. Claims that vitamin C will prevent, <u>relief</u>, or cure colds and winter illnesses are unwarranted, according to Hodges.
6. Magnesium deficiency is characterized by loss of appetite, nausea, <u>confusing</u>, loss of coordination, and tremors.

Exercise 5 *(page 121)*

1. Some people take vitamin E to relieve muscular cramps, to extend life span, and to *fight* skin problems.
2. The Nobel laureate Dr. Linus Pauling persistently claimed that vitamin C is effective in preventing and alleviating colds and *treating* cancer.
3. Many food processes such as drying, flavoring, canning, and *tenderizing* may add salt.
4. It is important to select foods that are in their best state, *store* them properly, and prepare them to ensure the maximum retention of vitamin C.
5. Avoiding the purchase of foods with salt content while marketing or *eating* out is helpful.
6. The major function of vitamin D is to ensure an adequate supply of calcium and phosphorus in the bones, to prevent rickets in children, and to *maintain* good levels of calcium and phosphorus in the blood.

Exercise 6 *(page 122)*

1. Very large intakes of any of the essential nutrients may result in both undesirable toxic symptoms and *serious* side effects.
2. Minerals in the cell influence not only the vital processes of oxidation but also *secretion* and growth.
3. Many people feel that both frozen and *canned* fruits and vegetables are inferior to fresh produce.
4. Canned food can neither be kept for unlimited lengths of time nor *be kept at* any temperature.
5. Fruit grown either sheltered from sunlight or *grown* in a season of many rainy days will not have much vitamin C.
6. Good peaches should be neither too hard, nor too *soft.*

Exercises on Parallel Structure

(page 123)
1. D
2. D
3. C
4. D
5. D
6. C
7. A
8. B
9. C
10. D
11. B
12. C

CHAPTER 14

Exercise 1 *(page 126)*

1. It is relatively easy for computers to speak.
2. Until recently it was thought computers would have to be programmed to the accent and speech habits of the user.
3. It is claimed that the IBM Tangora system can recognize a spoken vocabulary of 20,000 words.
4. Statistical probability is necessary for computers to interpret not only speech but visual data as well.
5. Up to now computers have not been programmed to react to a range of spoken commands.
6. The machine can calculate the probability of one particular word following another.

Exercise 2 *(page 126)*

1. Not until
2. Never
3. Not only
4. Not until
5. Only

Exercise 3 *(page 128)*

1. Should you make an error, it can be corrected easily.
2. On a magnetic disc information is stored.
3. Had he been more careful, we would not have lost all that data.
4. Not only does the computer store information, but also distributes it.
5. No sooner were personal computers invented than typewriters began to be replaced.
6. Only recently has the impact of the computer been strongly felt.

Exercise 4 *(page 130)*

1. D
2. B
3. B
4. D
5. B

Exercises on Word Order *(page 131)*
1. C
2. C
3. A
4. D
5. B
6. C
7. A
8. C
9. B
10. D
11. A
12. B

CHAPTER 15

Exercise 1 *(page 133)*
1. inventor/scientist
2. printer
3. politician
4. dangerous
5. thick metal
6. use

Exercise 2 *(page 134)*
1. F
2. F
3. T
4. T
5. T
6. T

Exercise 3 *(page 135)*
1. politician
2. inventor
3. science
4. printer
5. physicist
6. chemistry

Exercise 4 *(page 136)*
1. activate
2. thicken
3. sympathize
4. regularize, regulate
5. solidify
6. lighten

Exercise 5 *(page 136)*
1. entertainment
2. freedom
3. discovered
4. sign
5. service
6. developed

Exercise 6 *(page 138)*
1. successful
2. interested
3. weekly
4. safely
5. smokeless
6. good

Exercise 7 *(page 138)*
1. ADJ
2. N
3. N
4. N
5. ADJ
6. N/V
7. N
8. N
9. ADV
10. N

Exercise 8 *(page 139)*
1. ADJ
2. V
3. ADJ
4. ADV
5. N
6. V
7. N
8. ADJ

Exercises on Word Forms *(page 140)*
1. B
2. D
3. B
4. A
5. B
6. C
7. D
8. D
9. C
10. A
11. A
12. A

CHAPTER 16

Exercise 1 *(page 143)*
1. Unlike
2. so
3. After
4. almost
5. but
6. and

Exercise 2 *(page 143)*
1. B
2. A
3. D
4. E
5. C

Exercise 3 *(page 144)*
1. do, done, made
2. made
3. do
4. made
5. made
6. made

Exercise 4 *(page 145)*
1. Unlike
2. alike
3. Like
4. like
5. unlike
6. alike

Exercise 5 *(page 146)*
1. Another
2. other
3. another
4. other
5. Other
6. the other

Exercise 6 *(page 147)*
1. so
2. so
3. too
4. so
5. such
6. too

Exercise 7 *(page 148)*
1. Much
2. much
3. many
4. little, many
5. Few
6. little

Exercise 8 *(page 149)*
1. A number
2. Because of
3. not
4. After
5. some
6. most

Exercise 9 *(page 150)*
1. for example, such as
2. protect, guard
3. main, chief
4. Correct
5. Correct
6. unique, single
7. new, innovations
8. around, approximately

Exercises on Word Choice and Redundancy *(page 151)*
1. C
2. C
3. B
4. C
5. D
6. B
7. B
8. B
9. C
10. A
11. C
12. A

PRACTICE TEST 1 *(page 154)*
1. D
2. B
3. A
4. A
5. B
6. C
7. D
8. A
9. B
10. D
11. B
12. C
13. D
14. A
15. B
16. B
17. A
18. D
19. C
20. A
21. B
22. D
23. C
24. D
25. A
26. B
27. A
28. C
29. D
30. B
31. C
32. C
33. B
34. C
35. C
36. A
37. C
38. D
39. B
40. B

PRACTICE TEST 2 *(page 160)*

1. B
2. A
3. C
4. B
5. D
6. C
7. A
8. B
9. C
10. D
11. A
12. B
13. A
14. C
15. D
16. D
17. D
18. D
19. C
20. D
21. B
22. B
23. B
24. C
25. D
26. D
27. B
28. C
29. A
30. D
31. C
32. D
33. C
34. B
35. C
36. C
37. C
38. D
39. C
40. B

PRACTICE TEST 3 *(page 166)*

1. A
2. C
3. B
4. D
5. A
6. B
7. D
8. A
9. C
10. B
11. A
12. C
13. D
14. A
15. D
16. C
17. C
18. D
19. D
20. A
21. B
22. C
23. B
24. D
25. B
26. D
27. A
28. C
29. D
30. D
31. B
32. C
33. C
34. C
35. B
36. A
37. D
38. D
39. D
40. D

PRACTICE TEST 4 *(page 172)*

1. A
2. B
3. D
4. C
5. D
6. B
7. C
8. A
9. C
10. B
11. D
12. A
13. B
14. C
15. D
16. D
17. B
18. A
19. C
20. D
21. D
22. D
23. D
24. D
25. B
26. D
27. A
28. C
29. B
30. D
31. A
32. A
33. D
34. C
35. B
36. B
37. A
38. D
39. A
40. C

PRACTICE TEST 5 *(page 178)*

1. B
2. A
3. D
4. B
5. C
6. A
7. C
8. D
9. B
10. D
11. A
12. B
13. C
14. C
15. D
16. A
17. D
18. B
19. C
20. A
21. C
22. A
23. C
24. A
25. C
26. D
27. B
28. B
29. D
30. D
31. B
32. A
33. C
34. D
35. C
36. C
37. D
38. B
39. D
40. D

NOTES